Mayday Over America: The Delta Flight Tragedy

Table of Contents

Introduction 5

Chapter 1 The Last Takeoff 9

    1873: A Routine Journey 10

    The Crew and Passengers on Board 13

    Moments Before Disaster 16

    Air Traffic Control's Final Words 19

Chapter 2 The Mayday Call 23

    A Sudden Crisis at 30,000 Feet 24

    Captain's Desperate Decision 27

    The Race Against Time 29

    The Last Transmission 30

Chapter 3 The Tragic Descent 33

    The Mechanical Failure: What Went Wrong? 34

    Passengers' Final Moments 37

    The Chaos in the Cockpit 39

    The Impact and Immediate Aftermath 41

Chapter 4 First Responders and Rescue Efforts 44

    The Emergency Alert 45

Search and Recovery Operations 47

Survivor Stories and Eyewitness Accounts 49

The Nation Watches in Horror 52

Chapter 5 The Investigation Begins 54

NTSB and FAA Take Charge 55

Black Box and Voice Recordings 57

Theories and Initial Findings 60

Was This Preventable? 62

Chapter 6 Inside Delta Airlines 65

A History of Safety and Trust 66

Internal Reactions to the Tragedy 69

Crisis Management in the Spotlight 71

The Public Relations Nightmare 73

Chapter 7 The Families' Fight for Truth 76

The Grief of Lost Loved Ones 77

Demands for Justice and Accountability 80

Legal Battles Begin 82

The Power of Collective Action 85

Chapter 8 Unraveling the Technical Causes 88

The Aircraft's Maintenance History 90

Design Flaws and Possible Malfunctions 92

Expert Analyses and Disagreements 95

The Final Report 98

Chapter 9 The Legal and Political Fallout 102

Lawsuits Against Delta and Manufacturers 104

Congressional Hearings and Public Outcry 107

Changes in Aviation Policies 110

Airline Safety Reforms 113

Chapter 10 Could This Happen Again? 118

Lessons Learned from the Tragedy 120

Improvements in Aviation Safety 122

Preventing Future Disasters 126

Honoring the Lives Lost 129

Conclusion 131

Introduction

It was supposed to be just another routine flight. Delta Flight 1873, a well-maintained aircraft with an experienced crew, took off from its departure city with clear skies and an ordinary flight plan. Passengers settled into their seats, some engrossed in their books, others quietly conversing, while the hum of the engines provided a sense of reassurance. The cabin crew moved seamlessly through the aisles, attending to travelers, offering drinks, and ensuring everyone's comfort. For many, this was a journey like any other — a temporary space between departure and destination, where time slowed down in the altitude's stillness. But within hours, the ordinary became catastrophic.

Somewhere at cruising altitude, the first signs of trouble appeared. A sudden jolt, an unexpected vibration, and a series of warnings flashing in the cockpit signaled that something was terribly wrong. The pilots, seasoned professionals who had handled turbulence and technical hiccups before, initially remained calm. They worked through their checklists, troubleshooting the issue as they had been trained to do. Yet, as minutes passed, the situation rapidly deteriorated.

The air traffic control logs would later reveal the chilling words that marked the turning point. "Mayday, mayday, mayday. Delta 1873 declaring an emergency." The distress call, so rarely heard on commercial flights, sent immediate alarms through aviation networks. The pilots struggled to regain control of the aircraft, making desperate calculations, adjusting altitude, and searching for an emergency landing site. In the cabin, passengers began to realize the severity of the situation. Some clutched the armrests, others whispered prayers, and a few desperately dialed their loved ones, hoping for one last conversation.

Then, silence. The aircraft disappeared from radar, and within moments, a fiery explosion erupted on impact. News stations across the country interrupted programming, their screens flashing the words that no one ever wants to see: Breaking News: Delta Flight 1873 Down. The shockwaves from the tragedy rippled across the nation within minutes.

Air travel has long been considered one of the safest modes of transportation, with rigorous safety standards and advanced engineering minimizing risks. Yet, when disaster strikes, it shakes the collective consciousness of a nation. Americans, many of whom board planes daily for work, vacations, or reunions, were suddenly reminded of the fragility of human life in the vast skies above. The incident dominated every major news cycle. Images of smoldering wreckage, grief-stricken families, and aviation experts speculating on the possible causes filled television screens and news articles.

Airports became eerily somber as travelers, staring at flight information boards, wrestled with the fresh anxiety of stepping onto an aircraft. Airlines scrambled to reassure passengers, emphasizing their commitment to safety and pointing to the millions of uneventful flights that take place each year. Yet, beneath these reassurances was the undeniable truth—something had gone terribly wrong, and until investigators could determine why, no one would be at ease.

For the families of those on board, life changed in an instant. Loved ones who had left home that morning with casual goodbyes were now gone, their futures erased by a tragedy that could not yet be explained. Their grief was compounded by the unknown—what had happened? Was it mechanical failure? A lapse in maintenance? Pilot error? Was there a way this could have been prevented? The demand for answers became deafening, and as the first 24 hours passed, pressure mounted on aviation authorities to deliver an explanation.

With modern aviation disasters, the investigation begins the moment a plane goes down. Federal agencies, aviation experts, and safety boards moved quickly to assess the wreckage and retrieve the black boxes—the cockpit voice recorder and flight data recorder, the crucial pieces of evidence that would reveal the aircraft's final moments. Recovery teams scoured the crash site, meticulously gathering fragments of the plane, each twisted piece of metal holding a clue to the events that unfolded before impact.

Journalists, aviation analysts, and social media users speculated endlessly, dissecting every known fact, replaying radar data, and theorizing about what could have gone wrong. As officials from the National Transportation Safety Board (NTSB) took center stage in press conferences, they offered only preliminary findings, carefully avoiding assumptions. The investigation would take months, they warned, possibly even years. Every answer would need verification, every possibility explored.

But the world wasn't patient. Families wanted justice. The public demanded accountability. Airlines feared fallout. With each passing day, new questions emerged—had the aircraft been properly maintained? Had warnings been ignored? Was this part of a larger pattern of safety failures? And the most pressing question of all: Could this tragedy have been prevented?

In the following pages, this book will take you deep inside the story of Delta Flight 1873. It will examine the technical, human, and systemic factors that contributed to this disaster. It will explore the lives of those on board, the moments leading up to the crash, and the aftermath that followed. Most importantly, it will seek to answer a haunting question—how can we ensure this never happens again?

Chapter 1
The Last Takeoff

Delta Flight 1873 was scheduled for a routine departure, its flight plan meticulously mapped out, its aircraft inspected, and its crew briefed. It was a day like any other at the airport—passengers moving through security, grabbing last-minute snacks, and finding their seats before takeoff. The flight attendants greeted them with warm smiles, assisting travelers with their luggage and ensuring everyone was seated comfortably. The hum of boarding announcements and rolling suitcases filled the air, blending into the usual rhythm of air travel.

In the cockpit, Captain Mark Reynolds and First Officer Jason Keller performed their pre-flight checks, methodically verifying every system. Both were seasoned pilots, with thousands of hours of flight experience between them. The aircraft itself, a reliable model used by airlines worldwide, had passed all routine inspections. Nothing seemed out of the ordinary. The control tower gave final clearance, and the aircraft taxied onto the runway.

The engines roared to life as the plane accelerated down the tarmac. Passengers felt the familiar force pushing them back into their seats as the aircraft lifted gracefully into the sky. It was a smooth ascent, the kind pilots strive for, with minimal turbulence and clear weather ahead. Flight attendants made their rounds, ensuring everyone was settled and ready for the journey. The fasten-seatbelt sign dimmed, and the familiar chime signaled that the flight was proceeding as expected.

For many passengers, this was just another flight—some traveling for business, others reuniting with family, and a few embarking on long-awaited vacations. A couple seated near the wing held hands, exchanging quiet words. A businessman in first class typed furiously on his laptop. A mother adjusted her child's blanket, hoping for a peaceful journey ahead. Life continued as normal, with no indication of what was about to unfold.

At 30,000 feet, the pilots checked in with air traffic control, confirming a steady climb to cruising altitude. Everything seemed routine, but beneath the surface, something was amiss. Small, seemingly insignificant fluctuations in the aircraft's readings began to appear on the cockpit screens. The pilots noticed, made a mental note, and continued monitoring the systems. They had seen minor anomalies before—often, they amounted to nothing. But this time, something was different.

Then, it happened.

A sudden vibration. A slight jolt. A warning chime echoed through the cockpit. What had started as a routine takeoff had now shifted into the unknown. The pilots exchanged glances, their training kicking in as they prepared for what could become a life-or-death battle in the skies.

1873: A Routine Journey

Delta Flight 1873 was never meant to be anything more than an ordinary trip. It was a routine journey, the kind taken by thousands of passengers every day without a second thought. The aircraft was a widely used model, its maintenance records up to date, and the crew was composed of seasoned professionals who had logged thousands of hours in the skies. Everything about the flight, from the scheduled departure to the expected landing, was just another entry in Delta's daily operations.

The day began like any other at the airport. Travelers moved through security lines, some in a hurry to catch their connection, others leisurely sipping coffee as they waited to board. Business professionals checked emails on their phones, parents corralled their excited children, and flight attendants prepared the cabin for yet another uneventful trip. The passengers had little in common besides their shared destination, each with their own reasons for being aboard. Some were heading home, others setting off on long-awaited vacations, and a few were on business trips that, at the time, seemed like just another work obligation.

The crew, led by Captain Mark Reynolds and First Officer Jason Keller, performed their standard pre-flight checks. Reynolds was a respected pilot, known for his calm demeanor and sharp instincts. Keller, younger but equally skilled, had been flying commercial routes for nearly a decade. Both had seen their share of turbulence, emergency landings, and mechanical hiccups, but neither could have predicted what awaited them.

The aircraft itself, a workhorse of the airline's fleet, had undergone its routine inspections. Its systems checked out, its engines purred to life as the boarding process concluded, and soon, the aircraft was cleared for takeoff. Passengers settled into their seats, adjusting seatbelts and flipping through in-flight magazines. Some dozed off before the wheels even left the tarmac, while others stared out the windows as the ground below grew smaller. The takeoff was smooth, the ascent steady. Everything pointed to an uneventful flight.

At cruising altitude, the routine continued. Flight attendants moved down the aisles, offering drinks and snacks. Conversations hummed softly through the cabin, punctuated by the occasional laugh or the rustling of newspapers. The aircraft remained stable, gliding through the sky as though on an invisible track. The pilots exchanged brief updates with air traffic control, confirming their course and altitude. There were no storm warnings, no unexpected reroutes, nothing that would indicate trouble ahead.

But in aviation, routine can be deceptive. Even the most standard flights can change in an instant. Somewhere in the complex machinery of the aircraft, a system was beginning to fail. A small, unnoticed irregularity—one that hadn't raised alarms during the pre-flight inspection—was now setting off a chain reaction that would soon spiral beyond control. The passengers, unaware of the unfolding crisis, continued their journeys in the illusion of safety. Even the pilots, trained to recognize the earliest signs of trouble, had not yet detected what was happening.

The first indication of a problem came subtly, a minor fluctuation in one of the cockpit's instrument readings. Nothing alarming at first, just an anomaly that appeared and disappeared in the span of seconds. Perhaps a sensor glitch, Reynolds thought, making a mental note to monitor it. He glanced at Keller, who had noticed it too, but neither spoke. There was no reason to. Airplanes experience minor irregularities all the time—usually nothing to worry about.

Passengers remained blissfully unaware, engaged in their routines. Some scrolled through in-flight entertainment selections, others read books or closed their eyes for a mid-flight nap. In the galley, a flight attendant prepared coffee while another handed a child an extra packet of pretzels. It was the rhythm of travel, a dance perfected by airlines through decades of experience.

Then came the second anomaly. This time, it didn't disappear. A pressure warning flickered, then steadied into a bright red alert. Keller straightened in his seat, eyes scanning the instruments as Reynolds reached for the controls. They were still miles from their destination, still flying high above the clouds, but in that moment, everything changed.

What had begun as a routine journey was about to become anything but.

The Crew and Passengers on Board

Delta Flight 1873 carried a diverse group of people, each with their own destinations, plans, and lives waiting for them beyond the airport. From business executives and families on vacation to students, retirees, and airline crew members just doing their jobs, no one could have imagined that this flight would be their last. The passengers, seated in neat rows, represented different walks of life, yet in the final moments of the flight, they would share a single fate.

In the cockpit, Captain Mark Reynolds and First Officer Jason Keller were in command. Reynolds was a seasoned veteran with over twenty years of flying experience. Known for his calm demeanor and exceptional problem-solving skills, he had successfully handled difficult situations in the past, including emergency landings and mid-air technical malfunctions. His co-pilot, Keller, was younger but equally competent, having flown with Delta for nearly a decade. He was admired for his sharp instincts and quick thinking. The two had worked together before, developing a mutual trust that was essential in any cockpit. On this flight, they had expected nothing more than another routine journey, but their skills and decision-making would soon be put to the ultimate test.

Behind the closed cockpit doors, the flight attendants moved through the cabin, executing their duties with the efficiency and grace that comes with years of experience. Leading the cabin crew was Jessica Carter, the senior flight attendant, who had spent the past fifteen years ensuring passenger safety and comfort. She was joined by Emily Tran, a cheerful presence who had always dreamed of working in aviation, and Marcus Hill, a former military medic who had transitioned into commercial aviation. Their job was not only to serve drinks and snacks but also to maintain order, address passenger concerns, and, if necessary, act as first responders in emergencies.

Among the passengers, each seat held a different story. In seat 14A, an elderly couple, Robert and Anne Whitmore, were on their way to visit their grandchildren. It was a trip they had taken several times before, yet this one had felt especially exciting—Anne had just beaten cancer, and this was her first vacation in years. A few rows behind them, Maria Gomez, a single mother, sat with her five-year-old daughter, Sofia, who was eagerly looking out the window, pointing at the clouds and asking endless questions about how planes worked. Maria had promised her daughter a trip to Disney World, saving for months to make it happen.

In seat 22C, James "Jim" Holloway, a middle-aged sales executive, balanced his laptop on the tray table, typing furiously between sips of coffee. He had spent the morning finalizing a high-stakes deal and had boarded the plane thinking only about the contract he was about to close. Travel was a routine part of his job, and he barely noticed when the plane took off. In the row across from him, Danielle Richards, a college student, was returning home for summer break. She had spent the past semester abroad, immersing herself in new cultures and experiences, and she couldn't wait to see her family again.

Further back, in seat 30F, Sergeant Adam Lewis, a decorated Army veteran, sat quietly, looking out the window. He had been deployed three times overseas, had faced danger in combat zones, and had survived situations many would never understand. Flying didn't make him nervous—he had traveled in military transport planes, helicopters, and fighter jets. But today, for some reason, something felt off. It was a feeling he couldn't quite shake, an instinct honed from years in unpredictable situations.

In first class, Dr. Elaine Foster, a renowned neurosurgeon, enjoyed a rare moment of peace. She had just completed a grueling week of surgeries and was flying to attend a medical conference where she was scheduled to speak about advancements in brain trauma treatments. Across the aisle, Nathan Wells, a Wall Street investor, sipped his scotch, flipping through stock reports, completely absorbed in numbers and forecasts.

As the plane cruised through the sky, conversations hummed softly. Flight attendants moved effortlessly through the aisles, offering drinks and checking seat belts. The pilot's voice occasionally crackled through the speakers, reassuring passengers of a smooth flight and pleasant weather conditions.

Yet, in the cockpit, a different reality was unfolding. A warning light flickered on the instrument panel, unnoticed at first. Then, another. Captain Reynolds furrowed his brow, scanning the readings as Keller double-checked the aircraft's systems. The plane was cruising smoothly, but something wasn't right.

Back in the cabin, passengers laughed, chatted, and scrolled through their in-flight entertainment screens, oblivious to the growing tension behind the locked cockpit door. For the 187 souls aboard, life continued as normal, unaware that their routine flight had already begun its descent into disaster.

Moments Before Disaster

Delta Flight 1873 cruised smoothly at 35,000 feet, its passengers absorbed in their own worlds. Flight attendants moved through the aisles with practiced ease, offering drinks, adjusting blankets, and chatting with passengers. The hum of the engines was steady, the cabin lighting dimmed to a soft glow. There was no sign—at least to those in the cabin—that something was about to go terribly wrong.

In the cockpit, Captain Mark Reynolds and First Officer Jason Keller remained focused, their eyes flicking across the instruments as they monitored the aircraft's progress. The flight had been uneventful so far, just as expected. But then, a small indicator light flickered on the control panel. It was a minor alert—nothing immediately alarming. Reynolds took note of it but continued monitoring the plane's course. Keller glanced at him, as if to ask whether they should investigate further, but Reynolds gave a slight shake of his head. There was no need for concern yet.

Minutes later, another warning light appeared. This time, it stayed on. Reynolds adjusted his headset and reached for the controls, running a quick system check. The plane remained stable, but there was a slight, almost imperceptible vibration in the controls. Keller noticed it, too. He ran his fingers over the throttle, checking for any resistance, but everything still seemed operational. They were trained to handle turbulence, unexpected system glitches, and in-flight adjustments—but something about this felt different.

In the cabin, the passengers remained unaware. A mother held her sleeping child close to her chest, an elderly man adjusted his reading glasses to focus on the words of his book, and a group of teenagers whispered excitedly about their travel plans. Business travelers typed on their laptops, and a newlywed couple held hands, smiling as they planned their honeymoon itinerary.

Then, without warning, the first real sign of trouble struck. The plane suddenly shuddered—just for a second, but enough to catch attention. A few passengers looked up from their screens, but the moment passed so quickly that many dismissed it as turbulence. A flight attendant near the back of the cabin steadied herself against a seat, exchanging a glance with a colleague. It was common for flights to experience occasional rough air.

In the cockpit, however, things had escalated. The aircraft's hydraulic system was showing erratic readings, and Reynolds now felt resistance in the controls. He turned to Keller, who was already scanning through emergency checklists. They had trained for emergencies, but the data coming in didn't match any specific known failure. The aircraft wasn't responding normally, yet it wasn't completely failing either. The worst kind of problem was one they couldn't immediately diagnose.

The cockpit radio crackled. Air traffic control was checking in, confirming their position and flight path. Keller responded as if nothing was wrong, following protocol. The last thing they wanted was to cause panic prematurely. But inside the cockpit, their eyes told a different story. They were watching an issue develop in real time, and the plane was giving them less control with each passing second.

Then came the second jolt—more violent this time. The aircraft dipped slightly before stabilizing. Gasps rippled through the cabin. Flight attendants reassured nervous passengers, urging them to keep their seatbelts fastened. The turbulence explanation seemed reasonable enough, and most accepted it. But those who had flown frequently knew something was off. This wasn't turbulence—it felt mechanical.

Reynolds tightened his grip on the controls. The vibrations were growing stronger. Warning indicators continued to flash, and a sharp beeping noise signaled a deeper failure. Keller's hands moved swiftly over the switches, attempting to regain stability. The aircraft was still airborne, still functional, but it was slipping into the danger zone.

Back in the cabin, the shift in atmosphere was noticeable. Flight attendants exchanged glances, waiting for a message from the cockpit. A few passengers instinctively tightened their seatbelts. The once-casual conversations had faded, replaced by nervous whispers and worried looks.

Then, a chilling realization struck Reynolds. The plane wasn't just experiencing a system failure—it was losing control. His voice, calm but urgent, broke through the radio.

"Mayday, mayday, mayday. Delta 1873 declaring an emergency."

On the ground, air traffic controllers stiffened as they processed the distress call. Within seconds, emergency response teams were alerted.

In the cabin, the fasten-seatbelt sign flickered on, and flight attendants hurried to secure loose items. Passengers, sensing the change in energy, fell silent. Eyes darted toward the windows, toward the flight attendants, toward each other.

Then came the final, violent jolt. The aircraft suddenly dipped, throwing unbuckled passengers against their seats. Oxygen masks deployed as a deafening alarm sounded through the cockpit. The situation had spiraled out of control.

In those last moments before disaster, there was no more routine. No more certainty. Only fear, urgency, and a desperate fight to save the lives of those on board.

Air Traffic Control's Final Words

At the Atlanta Air Traffic Control Center, the routine monitoring of flight paths was uninterrupted, with controllers managing multiple aircraft at once. Delta Flight 1873 was just one of many flights on their radar that day, steadily moving along its assigned route. From their high-tech workstations, controllers ensured smooth transitions between airspace sectors, coordinating handoffs and maintaining safe separation between aircraft. It was another normal shift—until the call came in.

"Mayday, mayday, mayday. Delta 1873 declaring an emergency."

The voice of Captain Mark Reynolds came through, calm yet laced with urgency. Instantly, the controller overseeing Delta 1873 sat upright, signaling to his colleagues. In aviation, a mayday call meant one thing—life-threatening trouble.

"Delta 1873, state your emergency." The controller's voice remained steady, trained to remain professional even in moments of crisis.

There was a pause, static crackling over the frequency before Reynolds' voice returned. "We have a major system failure. Experiencing loss of control."

The words hit hard. Controllers were trained to handle all types of airborne situations—turbulence, reroutes, medical emergencies—but an aircraft losing control at cruising altitude was rare, and terrifying. Nearby, a supervisor had already tuned in, motioning for additional controllers to assist. In seconds, a response team gathered around the radar screen, their eyes fixed on Delta 1873's data.

The aircraft's altitude was dropping—slowly at first, then alarmingly fast. Numbers on the screen flickered as data points updated in real time.

The controller responded immediately, scanning the options. "Delta 1873, you are cleared to divert. Nearest airport is Birmingham. Can you maintain altitude?"

Reynolds' reply was garbled by interference, but they could make out enough. "Negative—losing power—controls are sluggish."

The tone in the room shifted. A sinking feeling spread through the team. They had seen planes recover from malfunctions before, but something about this was different. The data feed wasn't stabilizing. Delta 1873 was descending too fast.

The supervisor took over the microphone, his voice deliberate but firm. "Delta 1873, confirm souls on board. Do you require immediate emergency landing assistance?"

Another pause, then the chilling response: "187 souls on board. Unable to hold altitude. Request emergency guidance."

The room fell silent for a fraction of a second. Then, rapid movements—controllers calling emergency services, sending real-time updates to the FAA and NTSB, notifying fire and rescue teams. Every second mattered now.

"Delta 1873, we are working on emergency clearance. Keep us updated on control status."

No response.

"Delta 1873, do you copy?"

More static. Then, a strained voice—First Officer Jason Keller this time. "We're trying…to stabilize…losing hydraulics—"

The rest was lost in the garbled transmission. The descent rate increased. The aircraft was falling too fast, and the radar screen now showed altitude loss in rapid intervals. Controllers knew they were minutes, maybe even seconds, away from disaster.

"Delta 1873, if you can hear us, descend as smoothly as possible. We are standing by with emergency response."

Nothing.

A sharp, sudden blip on the radar.

Then, Delta Flight 1873 vanished from the screen.

For a moment, no one spoke. The room, which had been full of hurried voices and coordinated efforts, went completely still. Controllers stared at the blank space where Delta 1873's signal had been just seconds ago.

"Do we have any visuals?" The supervisor's voice broke the silence.

Another controller shook his head. "Last known position shows rapid descent. No further contact."

The air traffic control center went into full crisis mode. Emergency teams on the ground were dispatched to the aircraft's last known coordinates. Every attempt was made to reestablish communication. Calls were made to other pilots in the area to check for visual confirmation.

But deep down, they all knew.

Delta 1873 was gone.

Chapter 2
The Mayday Call

At first, the disturbance seemed minor—a subtle vibration, a flicker of an indicator light. Pilots Mark Reynolds and Jason Keller had both experienced mid-air turbulence, instrument glitches, and occasional system warnings before. But within seconds, the situation escalated. A sharp jolt shook the aircraft, followed by an unexpected drop in altitude. Alarm bells rang in the cockpit, and red warning messages flooded the flight control screens. Something was seriously wrong.

Reynolds immediately gripped the controls, trying to stabilize the aircraft. "What's going on?" Keller asked, his voice tense but controlled. The autopilot disengaged, forcing them to take full manual control. The aircraft wobbled as Reynolds fought against its sudden, erratic movements. The instrument panel showed a critical failure, but the exact cause remained unclear.

In the cabin, passengers felt the shift. The smooth ride had suddenly turned into an unsettling, uneven flight. Nervous murmurs spread among the rows as a second violent shake rattled the plane. Overhead compartments creaked, and a few seatbelts tightened against their occupants as the aircraft dipped lower. Flight attendants exchanged uneasy glances, gripping seatbacks for balance.

Reynolds knew they were in trouble. The aircraft was losing altitude too fast, and their control over it was slipping. Grabbing the radio, he made the call no pilot ever wants to make.

"Mayday, mayday, mayday. Delta 1873 declaring an emergency."

The distress call was received by air traffic control, triggering immediate protocol. "Delta 1873, state your emergency," the controller responded, his voice steady but urgent.

"We have a critical system failure—uncontrolled descent. Request emergency landing at nearest available airport," Reynolds replied, trying to keep his voice steady.

The controller acted fast, scanning nearby airports and clearing emergency runways. "Roger, Delta 1873. Diverting you to—" But before he could finish, another violent jolt rocked the plane. A loud bang echoed through the cabin. Passengers screamed. Oxygen masks dropped from the ceiling as the aircraft began a sharp, nose-down descent.

Keller struggled with the controls, his hands shaking as he attempted to assist Reynolds in regaining altitude. The aircraft was no longer responding as it should. "We're losing it," he muttered under his breath.

On the ground, air traffic control listened as static crackled over the radio. Then, the unthinkable—silence. Delta Flight 1873 had vanished from radar.

A Sudden Crisis at 30,000 Feet

At 30,000 feet, Delta Flight 1873 had settled into a routine cruise. The aircraft glided smoothly above the clouds, with no turbulence, no sign of trouble. In the cockpit, Captain Mark Reynolds and First Officer Jason Keller monitored their instruments, performing routine checks as they had done on countless flights before. The weather was clear, air traffic was light, and the flight was proceeding exactly as planned.

Then, without warning, the aircraft shuddered. It was subtle at first, just a slight vibration beneath the pilots' hands, but enough for both men to notice. Reynolds instinctively glanced at Keller, who was already scanning the instrument panel. A moment later, another tremor ran through the plane, this time more pronounced.

The cockpit display lit up with a flashing warning—a hydraulic system fault.

Hydraulic systems are the lifeblood of a commercial aircraft, controlling essential functions like steering, braking, and wing flaps. If the hydraulics failed, so did the pilots' ability to maintain control. Reynolds tightened his grip on the yoke, testing the plane's responsiveness. It still handled well, but the warning was persistent.

"Let's run diagnostics," Keller said, flipping through their emergency checklist. His voice was steady, but there was tension behind it.

Reynolds radioed air traffic control, keeping his tone calm. "Delta 1873 reporting a possible hydraulic issue. Request standby clearance."

Back in the cabin, passengers remained oblivious. A few had noticed the minor turbulence, but nothing about the flight seemed unusual. Flight attendants continued their rounds, serving drinks and adjusting blankets. A businessman in seat 22C kept typing on his laptop, unaware that just beyond the cockpit door, the pilots were engaged in a race against time.

Then the situation escalated dramatically.

The aircraft suddenly lurched to the left, jolting passengers and sending loose items flying. A few gasps rippled through the cabin, followed by nervous whispers. A flight attendant reached out to steady herself as the fasten-seatbelt sign dinged on.

In the cockpit, the controls resisted. The hydraulic failure wasn't just a warning anymore—it was happening in real-time. Reynolds fought against the yoke, but the plane was no longer responding the way it should.

"We're losing hydraulic pressure!" Keller shouted. His eyes darted between the pressure gauges, which were dropping fast.

Reynolds made a split-second decision. "Mayday, mayday, mayday! Delta 1873 declaring an emergency!"

His voice was clipped but controlled as he called out to air traffic control. On the ground, controllers immediately sprang into action, diverting nearby aircraft and clearing emergency runways.

Back in the cabin, panic spread as the aircraft dipped sharply. Oxygen masks dropped from the overhead compartments, and passengers screamed as the plane rattled violently. Flight attendants moved swiftly, instructing everyone to brace while fighting against the sheer force of gravity pressing them to the floor.

"Try to stabilize the descent!" Reynolds barked as he fought against the plane's nosedive.

Keller struggled to keep the engines balanced, but the controls refused to obey. They were locked in a battle they were losing. The cockpit filled with the sound of alarms blaring, the aircraft warning them of an impending stall.

For the 187 souls onboard, the routine flight had turned into a nightmare in a matter of minutes. Families clung to each other, strangers held hands, prayers and sobs mixed with the chaos. The pilots were doing everything they could, but the aircraft was no longer responding.

Then came one final jolt—a violent shudder that sent the plane into an uncontrollable spiral.

Delta 1873 was in freefall.

Captain's Desperate Decision

The cockpit of Delta Flight 1873 was a scene of chaos. Alarms blared, red warning lights flashed across the instrument panel, and the aircraft lurched violently with each passing second. Captain Mark Reynolds gripped the yoke with white-knuckled intensity, his instincts battling against a system that was failing him in real time. The plane was going down, and he had seconds to make a decision.

"We're losing hydraulic control! No response from the rudder!" First Officer Jason Keller shouted over the blaring alerts. His hands moved frantically across the controls, attempting to reroute power, but nothing was working.

The aircraft had already fallen below 20,000 feet, the rapid descent pushing passengers back into their seats as gravity intensified. In the cabin, people screamed and cried, oxygen masks swinging wildly from the ceiling as the plane trembled violently. The once-calm flight attendants were now shouting commands, bracing for the unknown.

Reynolds knew the window for recovery was closing fast. If they didn't regain some control over the aircraft immediately, there would be no chance of landing safely. His mind raced through his years of training. He had prepared for emergencies before, but not like this.

His options were few. With the hydraulic systems failing, they were losing command of the ailerons and elevators—the mechanisms responsible for controlling the plane's movement. Autopilot was useless, and manual control was slipping away.

Keller's voice cut through the chaos. "We need to divert—nearest airport is Birmingham! Can we make it?"

Reynolds scanned the instruments, calculating their descent rate. The aircraft was dropping too fast. They wouldn't make it to a major runway.

"Too far. We need open ground—now!" Reynolds responded, his voice firm, but beneath it was the weight of an impossible decision.

His eyes darted to the navigation display, searching for any safe stretch of land—a highway, a field, a river, anything that could act as an emergency landing zone. A commercial aircraft was not built for belly landings outside of a runway, but it was their only chance.

Reynolds made the call.

He pulled back slightly, trying to slow the descent, tilting the nose up just enough to give them some control. The engines roared as they struggled against the forces dragging the aircraft toward the ground.

He grabbed the radio. "Mayday! Delta 1873 attempting emergency landing. We need immediate emergency response at coordinates—"

His voice cut off in static.

In the cabin, passengers held onto their loved ones. Some prayed, others sobbed, and a few simply closed their eyes, bracing for the impact to come.

Reynolds locked eyes with Keller. No words were spoken—just a mutual understanding. This was it.

With one final adjustment, Reynolds committed to his last command as captain.

The ground rushed toward them.

The Race Against Time

The descent was no longer controlled—it was a freefall with a fight for survival. Inside the cockpit of Delta Flight 1873, Captain Mark Reynolds and First Officer Jason Keller were locked in a desperate battle against gravity, a failing aircraft, and the ticking seconds that separated them from impact. Every instrument was blaring alarms, every system designed to keep them safe was now failing, and the ground was coming up fast.

"We're out of time! We need to slow her down!" Keller shouted, sweat pouring down his face as he yanked at the unresponsive controls.

Reynolds barely had a moment to register his co-pilot's words. His mind was running on pure instinct, calculating the impossible— where to land, how to reduce speed, and how to keep the 187 souls on board alive. He knew that at this velocity, impact would be catastrophic unless they could stabilize the plane just enough for a survivable landing.

Below them, the terrain was a blur. Fields, forests, highways— none of them designed for an aircraft of this size. They had mere moments to find an open stretch of land that wouldn't tear the plane apart on contact. Air traffic control had gone silent, their last-ditch effort to relay coordinates lost in static. The crew was alone now.

In the cabin, chaos had taken over. Passengers screamed, sobbed, and clutched onto whatever they could. The fasten-seatbelt sign flickered erratically as the plane jerked violently from side to side. A flight attendant struggled to reach the intercom, her voice barely audible over the panic.

"Brace! Brace! Heads down! Stay down!"

Some obeyed instinctively, others were frozen in fear. Parents shielded their children. Strangers held hands. Time had slowed for them, even as the plane hurtled toward the ground.

Reynolds spotted a narrow clearing ahead—a stretch of land that, though not ideal, might give them a chance. He had one final maneuver to make.

"Cutting throttle! Deploying flaps—NOW!" he yelled.

Keller's hands flew across the switches, following orders even as the plane fought them every inch of the way. The hydraulics were barely responding, but the aircraft pitched slightly upward, slowing the descent just enough to reduce the fatal force of impact.

But it wasn't enough.

A deafening explosion of metal and earth erupted as the plane slammed into the ground, skidding across the landscape in a trail of fire, debris, and shattered lives.

And then—silence.

The Last Transmission

Inside the cockpit of Delta Flight 1873, Captain Mark Reynolds and First Officer Jason Keller fought with every ounce of skill and strength they had left. The aircraft was in its final descent, its systems failing, its controls barely responding. The alarms had become a constant, deafening wail, the cockpit lights flashing red, warning of what the pilots already knew—impact was imminent.

On the ground, air traffic controllers watched helplessly as the aircraft's altitude numbers plummeted. Every attempt to re-establish contact had failed. The plane was falling too fast, the radio crackling with static. Then, suddenly—a voice broke through.

"Mayday, Mayday! Delta 1873—"

The transmission was garbled, barely intelligible through the interference. The controllers leaned in closer, straining to make out the words.

Reynolds' voice was urgent but calm, the mark of a pilot trying to maintain control even in the face of an unavoidable catastrophe.

"We are... losing... all controls... Attempting emergency landing—"

Then—silence.

"Delta 1873, do you copy?" The lead controller's voice was sharp, desperate.

Nothing.

"Delta 1873, please respond!"

Still nothing. The radar screen showed a final, rapid descent—then the dreaded signal. The aircraft had disappeared. It was gone.

In the cabin, passengers braced for impact. Some whispered last prayers, others clutched loved ones, and a few simply closed their eyes, waiting for the inevitable.

Reynolds gripped the yoke one last time, Keller's hands moving instinctively alongside him, even though they both knew the outcome. The last transmission had been sent, and there was nothing left to say.

Then, with a final, thunderous impact, Delta 1873 met the earth.

In the air traffic control room, the static continued to hum, a ghost of the last words spoken before everything went dark.

Chapter 3
The Tragic Descent

Inside the cockpit of Delta Flight 1873, the situation had gone from bad to worse. The aircraft was now in a full-blown crisis, plummeting thousands of feet per minute. Captain Mark Reynolds and First Officer Jason Keller fought desperately to regain control, their hands firm on the yoke as alarms blared around them. The control panel was a sea of flashing red lights, warning of multiple system failures. The stick-shaker vibrated violently, signaling an impending stall.

"We're losing altitude too fast," Keller shouted over the deafening noise of the wind screaming outside the fuselage.

"Flaps to full! Try to level her out!" Reynolds commanded.

Keller reached for the controls, his fingers moving swiftly, but the aircraft barely responded. The engines were sputtering, unresponsive to throttle adjustments. The once-reliable machine was now fighting against them, each passing second bringing them closer to the ground.

In the cabin, sheer terror gripped the passengers. The violent descent had thrown some against their seats, while others clung desperately to armrests. The overhead compartments burst open, sending luggage crashing into the aisles. Children wailed, and adults shouted prayers, their faces pale with shock. The oxygen masks dangled, some swinging wildly from the force of the turbulence. A flight attendant struggled to reach the intercom but was thrown off balance as the plane lurched again.

The smell of burning fuel seeped into the cabin. Somewhere near the rear, a faint haze of smoke curled into the air, barely visible against the flashing emergency lights. The aircraft groaned under the stress, metal screeching as it fought against forces it was never designed to withstand.

"Come on, come on—" Reynolds gritted his teeth, trying one last maneuver to stabilize their descent. But it was no use. The ground was approaching too fast.

"Brace for impact!" Keller yelled into the intercom.

Passengers gripped their knees, heads down, as instructed. Some held hands, others whispered frantic last words. The reality of what was about to happen set in—this was no longer a fight for control. It was a fight for survival.

Then, a deafening roar. A final jolt.

The impact sent a shockwave through the earth. A massive explosion erupted on contact, sending fire and debris soaring into the sky. Delta Flight 1873 had met its tragic end.

And then, silence.

The Mechanical Failure: What Went Wrong?

Delta Flight 1873 had been a well-maintained aircraft, cleared for departure with no immediate concerns. But somewhere between takeoff and its sudden, catastrophic descent, a hidden failure emerged—one that would seal its fate before anyone realized what was happening. The investigation into the crash would later reveal a complex mechanical breakdown, one that raised troubling questions about airline safety, maintenance oversight, and whether this disaster could have been prevented.

The National Transportation Safety Board (NTSB), along with engineers from the Federal Aviation Administration (FAA) and aviation experts, meticulously examined the wreckage. Their first priority was recovering the flight data recorder (FDR) and the cockpit voice recorder (CVR)—the black boxes that would hold the key to understanding what had gone wrong. When the devices were retrieved, burned but intact, investigators knew they had a chance to piece together the final moments of Flight 1873.

Data from the black boxes painted a harrowing picture. The first indications of trouble had come at 30,000 feet, when the pilots noticed a sudden drop in hydraulic pressure. The aircraft's hydraulic systems controlled everything from rudder movement to wing flaps and landing gear—critical components that allowed the pilots to maintain stability in the air.

At first, the pressure loss was subtle, but within minutes, one of the three redundant hydraulic systems completely failed. A warning light flashed in the cockpit, but the aircraft was still flyable. Then, a chain reaction began. As the pilots attempted to troubleshoot the issue, a secondary failure in the remaining hydraulic lines sent the system into a downward spiral. The plane's ability to respond to pilot commands became delayed and sluggish.

Investigators discovered a rupture in one of the main hydraulic lines, likely caused by metal fatigue—a weakening of structural materials due to repeated stress over time. This kind of failure is rare, but not unheard of. In past aviation incidents, similar failures had led to catastrophic losses of control, often leaving pilots with limited or no ability to steer their aircraft.

Further analysis of maintenance logs revealed a troubling oversight. Just three months before the crash, the same aircraft had been flagged for anomalous hydraulic pressure readings. However, because the issue had been intermittent and hadn't triggered a full warning during routine inspections, it was marked as "non-critical" and left for future monitoring.

The final NTSB report would later confirm that the combination of metal fatigue, a misdiagnosed hydraulic issue, and a lack of immediate corrective action had contributed to the disaster.

The worst revelation was that, once the hydraulic system had failed completely, the pilots had been left with almost no control over the aircraft. Unlike modern fly-by-wire systems that allow for electronic backups, this aircraft relied heavily on hydraulic-assisted controls. Without them, Reynolds and Keller were fighting a battle they could never win.

As Flight 1873 plummeted, the pilots had tried everything—adjusting engine thrust, deploying emergency backup systems, even attempting to reroute the last remnants of hydraulic pressure to stabilize the descent. But the failure was too widespread, too fast.

By the time the aircraft had dropped below 10,000 feet, it was no longer responding to manual inputs. The pilots' final transmissions revealed their desperate efforts to find a safe place to land, but with no way to steer, their options were virtually nonexistent.

The final seconds before impact were recorded on the cockpit voice recorder. The pilots' voices remained calm, professional—even as the alarms screamed around them. Their last words were not of panic, but of determination, trying every last maneuver in an impossible situation.

Then, the black boxes went silent.

In the aftermath, aviation regulators would face tough questions. How had a known issue gone unresolved? Why hadn't additional maintenance been required? Could a backup hydraulic system have prevented this tragedy?

Delta Flight 1873 wasn't just a case of bad luck. It was a mechanical failure with warning signs that had been missed—a chilling reminder that even the safest airlines, the best pilots, and the most advanced aircraft are still vulnerable to the smallest overlooked detail.

Passengers' Final Moments

Inside the cabin of Delta Flight 1873, time seemed to slow as the aircraft descended uncontrollably. What had started as a routine flight had turned into a nightmare in mere minutes. The once-calm hum of the engines was now a deafening roar, the plane shuddering violently with every passing second. Passengers, who had been chatting, reading, or napping just moments before, now sat frozen in fear.

The first sign of real terror came when the overhead compartments popped open from the sudden jolt, sending bags tumbling into the aisles. A few passengers instinctively reached to grab their belongings before realizing—this wasn't turbulence. This was something much worse.

A loud crack echoed through the cabin as the plane tilted sharply to one side, forcing everyone to grip their armrests. Screams erupted as those who weren't wearing seatbelts were thrown forward, some colliding into the seats in front of them. A flight attendant, who had been collecting trash near the back, lost her footing and tumbled hard against the galley wall. Another grabbed onto a passenger's seat, her face pale, her breath ragged.

Then, the oxygen masks dropped from the ceiling.

The moment those yellow masks swung loose, reality set in. People began to panic. A mother desperately tried to put a mask over her young son's face, her hands trembling. A businessman, his laptop still open, fumbled to secure his own mask while simultaneously pressing the call button for a flight attendant. No one was answering those calls now.

Near the front of the plane, an elderly couple held hands, whispering to each other through their masks. Across the aisle, a college student clutched her phone, her fingers flying over the screen as she tried to send a message—one last text—before the connection was lost.

In first class, passengers who had spent the flight enjoying drinks and quiet conversations now sat in stunned silence. A doctor who had performed countless life-saving procedures in emergency rooms was now helpless. A retired pilot, who had flown commercial planes for decades, muttered a prayer, knowing full well that the pilots in the cockpit were fighting a losing battle.

The flight attendants, trained for emergencies but never truly prepared for something of this magnitude, tried to keep order. One of them, voice shaking, shouted over the noise, "Brace position! Heads down! Stay down!"

Some passengers obeyed instantly, hunching forward, arms over their heads. Others couldn't move, paralyzed with fear. Some screamed. Some sobbed. A few simply closed their eyes, waiting.

The plane lurched violently again, the descent now faster, more erratic. Through the windows, the clouds had disappeared, replaced by patches of green and brown—the land rushing toward them.

A young couple in the last row clung to each other, their hands locked so tightly their knuckles turned white. A man three rows ahead of them whispered, "It's okay, it's okay..." though no one knew if he was saying it for the others or himself.

A father in seat 18C turned to his teenage daughter. "I love you. No matter what happens, I love you." She nodded, tears streaming down her face, unable to speak.

Near the emergency exit, a woman pulled out her phone one last time. She pressed record and spoke softly. "If anyone finds this... please tell my family I love them. Tell my little girl I'm sorry."

The final seconds were filled with screams, prayers, gasps—until there was nothing left to say.

And then, with a deafening impact, the world went dark.

The Chaos in the Cockpit

In the cockpit of Delta Flight 1873, chaos reigned. The once-calm rhythm of an ordinary flight had dissolved into a nightmare, as alarms blared relentlessly, red and amber lights flashing across the instrument panel. Captain Mark Reynolds and First Officer Jason Keller were locked in a desperate struggle, their hands gripping the failing controls as they fought against the inevitable plunge toward the earth.

"We've lost hydraulics! No response from the rudder!" Keller shouted over the deafening sirens. His eyes darted between the failing instruments and the dizzying altitude readouts.

Reynolds didn't respond immediately. His mind was racing through emergency procedures, but nothing was working. The hydraulic pressure had collapsed completely, leaving them with barely any control over the aircraft's movements. They were flying blind, every command input yielding little to no response.

The aircraft lurched hard to the left, pitching downward as Keller fought to level it out. "Damn it, come on!" he muttered, straining against the yoke.

"Mayday, mayday! Delta 1873—we're losing control! Request immediate emergency landing!" Reynolds called into the radio, his voice strained but composed.

Static.

For a split second, they thought the transmission had gone unheard. Then, a voice crackled through.

"Delta 1873, state your altitude and heading—"

Before Reynolds could respond, the plane violently pitched forward. The sudden drop threw them against their seatbelts, their bodies slammed into the restraints as loose items in the cockpit flew into the air. The cockpit screamed with warnings—STALL, PULL UP, TERRAIN AHEAD.

"Engines still running, but they're not responding properly!" Keller yelled, gripping the throttle with both hands. He pushed forward, trying to force more power, but the engines were unresponsive—alive, but choked by the system failures cascading through the aircraft.

Reynolds' jaw clenched as he scanned the terrain ahead. They were too low, too fast. "We need a clearing! Somewhere to put her down!"

Keller's fingers flew over switches, flipping through emergency override sequences, but each attempt ended in failure. "We're not getting anything back! It's all frozen!"

"Come on, give me something to work with!" Reynolds growled, pulling back on the yoke, willing the aircraft to respond.

The control tower's voice cut through the static, but it was too late.

"Delta 1873, adjust heading immediately—"

The plane pitched again, harder than before, and this time it didn't recover.

The altitude numbers spun downward rapidly.

Keller turned to Reynolds, his eyes wide with the realization neither of them dared to speak.

They were out of time.

With one final desperate move, Reynolds cut power to the failing systems, hoping for a last-second stabilization. It never came.

The last thing recorded in the cockpit voice recorder was Keller's heavy breathing, Reynolds' fingers gripping the yoke, and the final, deafening alarm.

Then—impact.

The Impact and Immediate Aftermath

The moment of impact was catastrophic. Delta Flight 1873, out of control and plummeting at an impossible speed, slammed into the earth with a force that shattered metal, tore apart the fuselage, and sent a fireball erupting into the sky. The deafening explosion echoed for miles, a sickening contrast to the eerie silence that followed.

The aircraft, once a marvel of engineering, was now a twisted wreck of burning debris, scattered across the uneven terrain. The tail section had broken off on impact, flung several hundred feet from the rest of the fuselage. The wings, still partially intact, had been engulfed in flames, their fuel igniting into a raging inferno that consumed everything in its path. The nose of the plane had crumpled, crushed by the sheer velocity of the descent.

Inside what remained of the fuselage, the cabin was unrecognizable. Overhead compartments had torn free, their contents now part of the wreckage. The seats—those that hadn't been ripped from their bolts—were twisted at unnatural angles, their safety belts still fastened around lifeless passengers. Oxygen masks, once symbols of a desperate hope, now dangled uselessly, swaying in the heat of the flames.

For the few who had survived the initial impact, the scene was a nightmare beyond comprehension. Smoke filled what little remained of the air inside the broken cabin, choking the lungs of those still conscious. Fires raged in pockets throughout the wreckage, licking closer with every passing second.

A man near the emergency exit, dazed and bleeding, tried to move but couldn't—his leg was pinned beneath the collapsed ceiling panel. His breaths were ragged, the weight of debris pressing down on his chest. A few rows away, a woman stirred weakly, her head bleeding from the impact, her hand still gripping the seat in front of her as if bracing for a landing that never came.

Somewhere in the wreckage, a faint cry for help pierced the silence.

Outside, witnesses rushed toward the flames, their eyes wide with horror. Drivers on a nearby highway had seen the fiery descent, their cars now pulled over haphazardly as they ran toward the smoldering remains. Some held their phones, frantically dialing 911, screaming to dispatchers that a plane had gone down.

Emergency services were already on the way. Fire trucks, ambulances, and police raced toward the site, their sirens blaring through the thickening smoke. Every second mattered, but for many inside the wreckage, time had already run out.

As first responders arrived, they braced themselves for what they knew would be one of the worst aviation disasters in recent history. What they found was a scene of destruction, death, and the faintest glimmer of life clinging on.

The rescue operation had begun, but for most of the 187 souls aboard Delta Flight 1873, the journey had already come to its tragic end.

Chapter 4
First Responders and Rescue Efforts

The explosion could be seen for miles. A massive fireball lit up the sky, and a thick column of black smoke spiraled upward, marking the tragic end of Delta Flight 1873. Within minutes, emergency dispatch centers were flooded with calls from witnesses—locals who had seen the aircraft go down, truck drivers who had spotted the fireball on the highway, and even air traffic control personnel who had lost the plane from radar. The coordinates were quickly relayed to first responders, setting off a desperate race against time.

Fire trucks, ambulances, and law enforcement vehicles roared toward the crash site, their sirens piercing the air. Local fire departments, along with state emergency services, mobilized every available unit. The closest responders, a rural fire department stationed just miles from the impact zone, were the first to arrive. As they approached, the heat was almost unbearable. The flames were raging, consuming the remnants of the aircraft. The once-intact fuselage was now a shattered wreck, scattered across a vast debris field. Smoke choked the air, making visibility nearly impossible.

Firefighters immediately began battling the inferno, deploying foam suppressants to smother the jet fuel-fed flames. They worked tirelessly, their protective gear drenched in sweat, knowing that every second counted. The goal was twofold—contain the fire and search for survivors. But the wreckage was unrecognizable, twisted metal and charred remains making the task feel insurmountable.

In the midst of the chaos, paramedics and emergency medical personnel rushed to locate any signs of life. They combed through the wreckage, listening for voices, for movement, for anything. The haunting silence was broken only by the crackling of flames and the occasional collapse of weakened metal structures. As daylight faded, portable floodlights illuminated the site, allowing the search to continue.

Law enforcement officers quickly secured the perimeter, keeping anxious onlookers and news crews at bay. Federal agencies, including the National Transportation Safety Board (NTSB) and the Federal Aviation Administration (FAA), were en route, preparing to take control of the investigation.

By the time the fire was subdued, the grim reality had set in. There were no survivors. The first responders, hardened by years of emergency response, stood in solemn silence as the weight of the tragedy bore down on them. Some bowed their heads in respect. Others whispered prayers. The rescue mission had become a recovery operation.

And as the nation watched, grief and shock spread like wildfire. Delta Flight 1873 was gone, leaving behind devastation, unanswered questions, and a country in mourning.

The Emergency Alert

The first 911 calls flooded in within seconds of the crash. Drivers on the nearby highway, residents in distant farmhouses, and air traffic controllers who had lost Delta Flight 1873 from radar all reported the same thing—a massive explosion, a fireball in the sky, and a deafening impact that shook the ground.

Inside emergency dispatch centers, alarms blared as operators worked swiftly to coordinate responses. Calls came from witnesses screaming about a plane going down, some describing a "giant fire near the fields," others panicked and uncertain of what they had just seen. The scale of the disaster was immediately clear.

"We have an aircraft down. We need all available fire and medical units dispatched immediately!" a dispatcher called out over the emergency radio.

Fire trucks, ambulances, and police vehicles from multiple jurisdictions tore through the streets toward the last reported location of the crash. Air traffic control confirmed that Delta 1873 had vanished from radar—no distress call had followed, no last-second correction. The aircraft had gone down, and the only question now was whether anyone had survived.

As first responders neared the impact site, they could already see thick black smoke billowing into the sky. Flames still raged from what remained of the wreckage, and the smell of burning fuel and metal hung heavy in the air.

"Jesus... It's worse than we thought," one firefighter muttered as his truck pulled up to the scene.

From the command center, the fire chief quickly assessed the situation. "We have a mass casualty incident. Get search-and-rescue teams deployed!" Over the radio, more fire stations were called in. Helicopters were dispatched for aerial surveillance, relaying real-time images of the devastation to emergency crews on the ground.

Police officers secured a perimeter around the wreckage, keeping civilians and media back while emergency workers rushed forward. Paramedics, carrying stretchers and trauma kits, sprinted toward any sign of movement among the debris.

"We have possible survivors!" a rescuer shouted.

Firefighters worked against the clock, trying to contain the flames before they reached any potential survivors. Hydraulic rescue tools were deployed to pry open twisted metal, while others worked frantically to extinguish burning fuel.

Airline officials had also been notified. Delta Airlines' crisis team activated its emergency protocol, alerting corporate leadership and mobilizing a response team. Within minutes, their spokesperson was on the phone with authorities, trying to gather any information on survivors, cause, and immediate next steps.

In hospitals nearby, emergency rooms prepared for incoming casualties. Trauma surgeons were called in early, burn units put on high alert. But no one knew how many survivors there would be—if any.

The scale of the disaster was becoming clearer by the second. The world had just lost a commercial flight, and the emergency response had only begun.

Search and Recovery Operations

The search and recovery operation for Delta Flight 1873 began the moment the wreckage was located. Emergency responders arrived at the scene within minutes of the crash, but what they found was a landscape of devastation. The aircraft had broken apart on impact, its fuselage shattered and burning, with debris scattered over a vast field. The once-pristine cabin was now a smoldering wreck, torn open by the force of the crash.

The first responders moved quickly, knowing that every second counted. Firefighters fought against the intense flames, battling to extinguish the jet fuel-fed inferno. The heat was overwhelming, making it nearly impossible to reach certain sections of the wreckage. Smoke choked the air, reducing visibility, while small explosions from ruptured fuel lines forced crews to stay on high alert.

Among the wreckage, the priority was finding survivors. Paramedics rushed toward any sign of movement, voices, or breathing. Miraculously, a few passengers were found alive, trapped under twisted metal and scattered debris. A firefighter spotted a hand reaching through a crack in the wreckage, weakly grasping at the air.

"We've got a live one!" he shouted, and within moments, a team of rescuers descended to pull the injured passenger from the debris.

Further into the wreckage, paramedics discovered a flight attendant, barely conscious but alive, wedged between two collapsed sections of the fuselage. She was covered in burns and lacerations, her uniform torn, but she was breathing.

With medical helicopters on standby, survivors were quickly stabilized on the ground before being airlifted to the nearest trauma centers. Every moment mattered—their conditions were critical, and the window for survival was closing.

As the fire teams controlled the remaining flames, recovery crews began searching for bodies. The heartbreaking task of locating and identifying the deceased was underway. Rows of white sheets were laid out on the ground, each one covering a life lost. Investigators from the National Transportation Safety Board (NTSB) and Federal

Aviation Administration (FAA) arrived at the scene, setting up a makeshift command center. Their first objective: locate the black boxes, the cockpit voice recorder (CVR) and flight data recorder (FDR)—the keys to understanding what had happened in the final moments of the flight.

Search teams meticulously combed through the wreckage, using specialized equipment to detect electronic signals. After hours of searching, a crew member shouted the discovery that investigators had been waiting for—

"We've got the black boxes!"

Burned but intact, the two critical devices were recovered and rushed to NTSB headquarters for analysis. They held the last words spoken in the cockpit and the vital data that could explain the cause of the crash.

As night fell over the crash site, search lights illuminated the grim scene. Forensic teams began the painstaking process of identifying victims, a task that would take weeks. Family members of the passengers were already gathering at airports, desperate for news. Delta Airlines' crisis team coordinated with authorities, setting up grief counseling services and arranging for families to be transported to the site.

For many, the search and recovery was only the beginning. The next steps—understanding why this happened and ensuring it never happened again—were just beginning.

Survivor Stories and Eyewitness Accounts

The story of Delta Flight 1873 was, for most on board, one that ended in tragedy. But against all odds, some survived, pulled from the wreckage by first responders or emerging from the twisted remains of the fuselage. Their accounts, along with those of witnesses on the ground, would help piece together the final moments of the doomed flight.

For Emily Tran, a flight attendant seated in the rear galley, the last thing she remembered before impact was gripping the jump seat harness as the aircraft nosedived. The plane shook so violently she thought it would tear apart in the air. One moment they were flying, and the next, it felt like they had no control. When the plane hit the ground, Emily was thrown against the side of the cabin, her body pinned by collapsed metal and burning debris. She blacked out. Hours later, she awoke to the sound of firefighters calling out for survivors. Rescuers pulled her free, her body covered in burns, her uniform singed beyond recognition.

Another survivor, James Holloway, a businessman in seat 22C, had been working on his laptop when the aircraft lurched. He remembers the screams as the oxygen masks deployed, the sheer helplessness as the plane plummeted. He tried to brace, but everything was moving so fast, like the world had been turned upside down. Then… nothing. James was one of the few pulled from the main wreckage alive, though his injuries were severe. When he came to, he smelled fuel and fire. He knew he had to get out, but he couldn't move his legs. First responders carried him from the wreckage, barely escaping before the flames consumed what was left of the fuselage.

Perhaps the most haunting story came from Sofia Gomez, a five-year-old girl, found clutching a stuffed animal near the broken wing section. She had been sitting with her mother, Maria Gomez, who didn't survive the crash. A firefighter carried Sofia away from the burning wreckage, the little girl too stunned to cry. She simply whispered, "Mommy's sleeping."

For those on the ground, the sight of a massive commercial airliner spiraling downward was something they would never forget. David Michaels, a truck driver on the highway near the crash site, saw the plane coming in low, trailing smoke. It was barely staying level. The wings wobbled, and then it just—dropped. He pulled over immediately, calling 911.

Another witness, Linda Carpenter, was outside her farmhouse when she heard a thunderous roar overhead. She looked up and saw this huge plane, way too low, moving erratically. She knew something was wrong. Seconds later, there was an explosion that shook the ground.

Several local residents rushed toward the wreckage before emergency responders arrived, but the heat was too intense to get close. Some could hear voices, people calling for help, but the fire was everywhere. The screams would stay with them forever.

The survivors, though grateful to be alive, were left with unimaginable trauma. Some suffered severe burns, broken bones, and internal injuries, but the psychological scars ran even deeper. Many would later speak of survivor's guilt, struggling to understand why they had lived when so many others had not.

For the eyewitnesses who had seen Delta Flight 1873's final moments, the horror of that day would stay with them forever. The image of the falling plane, the moment of impact, the helplessness of standing on the ground watching it happen—all of it etched into their memory.

Their stories, along with the black box recordings, became part of the larger investigation. The details they provided helped reconstruct the final moments of Delta 1873, ensuring that the world never forgot what happened that day.

The Nation Watches in Horror

News of the Delta Flight 1873 crash spread with shocking speed, sending ripples of fear and heartbreak across the nation. Within minutes of the impact, live coverage dominated television screens, social media feeds were flooded with speculation and desperate pleas for information, and a growing crowd gathered at airports, waiting for news of their loved ones. The nation was watching in horror, gripped by the unfolding tragedy.

At Delta Airlines' headquarters, executives scrambled to respond. Crisis management teams worked around the clock, drafting statements and fielding calls from frantic family members demanding answers. At major airports, including the flight's intended destination, grief-stricken relatives stood in stunned silence, staring at the departure board where "ON TIME" had changed to "CANCELLED." Some still clung to hope, praying it was a mistake. Others collapsed in sobs as the realization set in—their loved ones were gone.

Major news networks interrupted their regular programming with breaking news banners flashing across the screen. The words "PLANE DOWN: DELTA FLIGHT 1873 CRASHES" dominated the headlines. Reporters, barely able to keep up with the flood of information, stood near airports, at the crash site, or outside the National Transportation Safety Board (NTSB) offices, delivering grim updates. Experts speculated on the possible causes, with aviation analysts discussing past crashes, mechanical failures, and the difficulties pilots face when systems fail midair.

Social media became a virtual town square of grief and speculation. The hashtags #Delta1873, #PrayForPassengers, and #Flight1873Crash trended within minutes. Some users shared photos and videos of the plane's final descent, captured by horrified onlookers. Others expressed condolences to the families, while some demanded immediate answers from Delta Airlines, the Federal Aviation Administration (FAA), and the NTSB. Conspiracy theories also emerged, with speculation ranging from terrorism to aircraft malfunctions that had been ignored.

The White House released a statement from the President, offering condolences to the victims' families and promising a full investigation into the disaster. Lawmakers called for urgent aviation safety hearings, vowing that if negligence played a role in the crash, those responsible would be held accountable.

In the days following the tragedy, memorial vigils were held across the country. Candles were lit outside airports, photos of passengers were placed at makeshift memorials, and the names of those lost were read aloud in somber ceremonies. Schools, businesses, and entire communities mourned those they had lost, struggling to process the magnitude of the event.

The crash of Delta Flight 1873 had shaken the nation. Every detail, every survivor's account, every update from investigators was followed with intense scrutiny. Americans had seen aviation disasters before, but each time, the pain felt fresh. The questions remained — how did this happen, and could it have been prevented? The entire country waited for answers, watching as investigators combed through the wreckage, hoping that this tragedy would not become just another headline lost in time.

Chapter 5
The Investigation Begins

As the sun rose over the crash site of Delta Flight 1873, a grim silence settled over the smoldering wreckage. The once-bustling field of first responders had transitioned into a carefully controlled crime scene, with investigators methodically stepping through the debris, taking photographs, and marking evidence. The National Transportation Safety Board (NTSB) had officially taken over, launching what would become one of the most scrutinized air disaster investigations in recent history.

Within hours of the crash, federal agents from the NTSB, the Federal Aviation Administration (FAA), and representatives from Delta Airlines arrived at the site, joining local law enforcement and emergency personnel. The immediate priority was recovering the black boxes—the cockpit voice recorder (CVR) and the flight data recorder (FDR). These crucial pieces of equipment, built to withstand extreme impacts, were the best hope for unraveling the mystery behind the catastrophe.

It didn't take long for recovery teams to locate the black boxes amidst the wreckage. Though charred, they appeared intact—an initial relief to the investigators. The devices were rushed to NTSB's headquarters, where forensic analysts would painstakingly extract the final moments of flight data and the pilots' conversations.

Meanwhile, at the crash site, investigators examined the aircraft's fuselage, looking for telltale signs of mechanical failure, structural fatigue, or external impact. Sections of the plane were carefully tagged and transported for further analysis. Engineers scrutinized every detail, from the engines to the hydraulic systems, searching for an explanation.

Back at Delta's headquarters, company executives were in crisis mode. The airline's safety record was under the microscope, and public trust was at stake. A team of aviation experts reviewed the aircraft's maintenance logs, hoping to determine whether any recent repairs or reported issues might have played a role in the disaster.

As media outlets broadcast live coverage, speculation ran wild. Some experts pointed to mechanical failure, while others suggested pilot error or weather-related complications. A few even raised concerns about possible sabotage or cybersecurity vulnerabilities in modern aircraft systems. The public wanted answers, but the NTSB warned that a full investigation could take months—perhaps even years.

Families of the victims demanded accountability. They wanted to know what had caused the tragedy and whether it could have been prevented. And so, the painstaking process of uncovering the truth began—one data point, one wreckage fragment, one black box recording at a time.

NTSB and FAA Take Charge

The investigation into Delta Flight 1873 began within hours of the crash, as the National Transportation Safety Board (NTSB) and the Federal Aviation Administration (FAA) moved swiftly to take control of the scene. Their task was daunting—to determine what went wrong, how it happened, and whether it could have been prevented. Every air disaster carries lessons, and the agencies were under immense pressure to uncover the truth.

At the crash site, NTSB investigators arrived in specialized gear, surveying the wreckage in the early dawn light. Charred debris stretched for hundreds of yards, the aircraft barely recognizable. First responders had already done their part—rescuing survivors, extinguishing fires, and securing the area. Now, it was the investigators' turn.

Their first priority was recovering the black boxes—the cockpit voice recorder (CVR) and the flight data recorder (FDR). These two devices held the most critical clues to the final moments of Flight 1873. Teams scoured the wreckage, knowing that these recorders were designed to withstand even the most violent impacts. When the charred boxes were found—battered but intact—they were immediately transported to NTSB headquarters for analysis.

Simultaneously, FAA officials launched their own inquiry. Their role was to examine whether airline policies, maintenance records, and regulatory compliance had played any role in the disaster. Delta Airlines was required to submit detailed maintenance logs, crew training histories, and prior incident reports involving the aircraft. Investigators wanted to know:

1. Had there been previous reports of mechanical issues?
2. Were any known defects ignored or dismissed as minor?
3. Had the pilots received adequate training for emergency scenarios like this?

As NTSB experts reconstructed the final moments of the flight, they also worked with aviation engineers to examine pieces of the wreckage. The investigation team carefully tagged and collected sections of the fuselage, hydraulic components, and engine parts to determine whether mechanical failure, human error, or environmental factors had contributed to the crash.

At a press conference, the NTSB chair reassured the public that no stone would be left unturned. Reporters fired questions, eager for immediate answers, but investigators cautioned that the full report could take months or even years to complete. Families of the victims, desperate for closure, were left waiting in anguish.

As public pressure mounted, Congress announced hearings on aviation safety, summoning officials from the FAA, Delta Airlines, and aircraft manufacturers to testify. Lawmakers demanded answers about maintenance regulations, oversight failures, and whether systemic issues in the airline industry had played a role in the tragedy.

Meanwhile, the black box analysis revealed chilling details. The cockpit voice recorder captured the pilots' final desperate moments, while the flight data recorder confirmed a catastrophic hydraulic failure that left the crew with little to no control over the aircraft.

With each new revelation, it became clear that Delta Flight 1873 was not just a random accident. Something had gone terribly wrong—and now, the NTSB and FAA were tasked with ensuring that it never happened again.

Black Box and Voice Recordings

The cockpit voice recorder (CVR) and flight data recorder (FDR)—commonly known as the black boxes—were the key to understanding what had truly happened aboard Delta Flight 1873. Despite the intense impact and fire, the recorders were designed to survive extreme conditions, and their recovery was a critical breakthrough in the investigation. NTSB analysts rushed them to their Washington, D.C. headquarters, where teams of specialists would meticulously extract the data that could provide the final moments of the flight.

The flight data recorder was the first to be analyzed. It contained thousands of parameters tracking the aircraft's speed, altitude, control inputs, and system functionality. Investigators combed through the data, reconstructing the timeline of failure that had started at 30,000 feet. The readings confirmed the worst fears—a total hydraulic system failure had crippled the aircraft, rendering it nearly impossible to control. The data showed the pilots' frantic attempts to stabilize the plane, including emergency maneuvers, last-ditch adjustments to engine thrust, and repeated inputs to override failing systems. But nothing had worked.

The cockpit voice recorder was even more chilling. Investigators listened in absolute silence as the last conversations of Captain Mark Reynolds and First Officer Jason Keller played back. At first, their voices were calm and methodical—routine checks, altitude adjustments, radio confirmations. But then came the first warning chime, followed by Reynolds' voice:

"We've got a pressure drop—check hydraulics."

A few minutes later, Keller's tone had changed, sharper now.

"We're losing control authority. No response on the rudder—what the hell's happening?"

The static-filled response from air traffic control came next, asking them to state their emergency. Reynolds responded, his voice still steady, though laced with urgency:

"Mayday, mayday, mayday. Delta 1873. We have a major system failure—controls are unresponsive."

A loud shuddering sound filled the recording, followed by alarms. Then, an explosion-like noise, likely the hydraulic system rupturing completely. The plane pitched violently, and the voices became more frantic.

Keller: *"We're rolling left—no response, no response!"*

Reynolds: *"Damn it—come on, stay with me!"*

In the background, a chorus of warning alarms overlapped—the stall warning, ground proximity alert, and the repeated electronic voice: *"Terrain, terrain—pull up!"*

Then came one final transmission from Reynolds. His voice, though strained, was calm—the last act of a captain trying to save his crew and passengers.

"Brace for impact."

A deafening static burst, followed by the screech of metal, and then—silence.

Investigators sat in heavy silence, knowing they had just listened to the final seconds of 187 lives. The pilots had fought until the very end, but the failure was too severe, too sudden, too unstoppable.

The recordings were later played for the families of the victims in a private session, where grief, anger, and heartbreak filled the room. Some clung to the knowledge that their loved ones had not died without a fight, that the crew had done everything humanly possible to save them.

For the NTSB and FAA, the black box recordings were damning. The failure that had doomed Flight 1873 was not just a tragic accident, but a mechanical catastrophe that raised serious questions. Had maintenance protocols been ignored? Could this have been prevented?

The answers were still unfolding, but one thing was certain—the last words of Delta Flight 1873 would not be forgotten.

Theories and Initial Findings

As investigators pieced together the final moments of Delta Flight 1873, a series of theories emerged, each attempting to explain the catastrophic failure that led to the crash. The National Transportation Safety Board (NTSB), in collaboration with the Federal Aviation Administration (FAA), airline officials, and aviation experts, worked tirelessly to uncover the truth. With the black box data analyzed, wreckage examined, and maintenance logs scrutinized, the early findings began to reveal a chilling sequence of events.

One of the first theories centered around mechanical failure, specifically a hydraulic system collapse. Data from the flight data recorder (FDR) showed that the primary and backup hydraulic systems had lost pressure almost simultaneously, leaving the pilots with limited or no control over the aircraft's movement. This raised immediate concerns—how did two redundant systems fail at the same time? Investigators suspected a rupture in a critical hydraulic line, possibly due to metal fatigue, poor maintenance, or a manufacturing defect.

Another theory involved pilot error, though early evidence suggested Captain Mark Reynolds and First Officer Jason Keller had done everything possible to save the aircraft. Some speculated whether the crew had responded incorrectly to the hydraulic failure, but cockpit recordings indicated that they followed emergency protocols precisely. Investigators found no evidence of miscalculations, delayed reactions, or human-induced errors.

There was also a possibility of sabotage or terrorism, a theory that gained traction in the media in the days following the crash. However, forensic investigators found no traces of explosive residue, and intelligence agencies reported no credible threats against the flight. Security footage and passenger manifests were reviewed thoroughly, and no suspicious activity was found in pre-flight security checks.

Another line of inquiry pointed toward weather conditions, but analysis confirmed that Delta 1873 had been flying in clear skies with no turbulence or severe storms at the time of the failure. Weather was ruled out early in the investigation as a contributing factor.

The final and most concerning theory involved a critical design flaw or overlooked maintenance issue. Maintenance logs showed that this particular aircraft had reported intermittent hydraulic system warnings in previous flights. However, these warnings had been categorized as non-critical and deferred for further monitoring. Investigators began to focus on whether this was a case of negligence—either from the airline, the maintenance crew, or the aircraft manufacturer.

As the wreckage analysis continued, metal fragments from the hydraulic system were recovered, showing signs of stress fractures and potential failure points. A metallurgical examination suggested the possibility of a slow-developing fatigue crack in a critical pressure line, which, if ruptured mid-flight, could have caused a rapid hydraulic failure.

Another major finding was that the aircraft's emergency backup controls had failed to engage properly, meaning the pilots had been left without even the most basic maneuvering capability. This raised questions about whether the aircraft manufacturer had tested its emergency control systems under real-world conditions.

The black box recordings confirmed that the pilots had fought until the very last moment, attempting every possible maneuver to stabilize the plane. They had attempted manual control overrides, using differential engine thrust to try and guide the plane, but nothing had worked.

By the end of the initial investigation phase, the most likely cause of the crash was identified as a catastrophic hydraulic system failure, worsened by a pre-existing mechanical defect that had gone undetected—or worse, ignored. Investigators suspected that maintenance delays and potential cost-cutting measures may have played a role, setting the stage for a legal and political firestorm.

The nation waited anxiously for the final report, but the early findings already pointed to systemic failures—failures that had cost 187 lives.

Was This Preventable?

As the National Transportation Safety Board (NTSB) and Federal Aviation Administration (FAA) sifted through the wreckage and analyzed the flight data, one question loomed over the entire investigation: Could the crash of Delta Flight 1873 have been prevented? The more evidence investigators uncovered, the more it became clear that this was not a case of bad luck or an unavoidable disaster. The warning signs had been there all along, but they had either been overlooked, misjudged, or ignored.

Maintenance records showed that the aircraft had a history of hydraulic system inconsistencies, with multiple reports of fluctuating pressure levels in recent months. These warnings, however, were dismissed as minor issues, with technicians marking them for "further observation" rather than immediate repair. This raised serious concerns among investigators—if a critical component like the hydraulic system had shown signs of failure before, why had Delta Airlines and its maintenance crews not acted sooner? Was it a failure of protocol, a lapse in oversight, or a decision based on cost-cutting and operational efficiency?

Further examination revealed design vulnerabilities in the hydraulic system itself. The aircraft model had three redundant hydraulic systems, meant to ensure that even if one failed, the other two would provide control. But in this case, all three systems suffered cascading failures, leaving the pilots helpless. Metallurgical analysis of the wreckage confirmed stress fractures in a key hydraulic line, likely caused by prolonged wear and tear. The rupture had likely triggered a rapid loss of pressure, sending the aircraft into an uncontrollable descent. This led experts to question whether the aircraft manufacturer had sufficiently tested its hydraulic systems under real-world stress conditions.

The cockpit voice recorder (CVR) provided further damning evidence. Captain Mark Reynolds and First Officer Jason Keller had followed every emergency protocol, trying to reroute pressure, deploy manual control backups, and even use engine thrust for maneuvering. But with complete hydraulic failure, their options were almost nonexistent. The pilots had no way to save the flight, despite their best efforts. The fatal flaw had been mechanical, not human.

Regulatory agencies faced growing scrutiny. The FAA, responsible for enforcing airline safety standards, had approved multiple deferred maintenance reports on this aircraft, allowing it to remain in service despite past hydraulic warnings. Lawmakers demanded answers: Had safety standards been compromised for operational convenience? Had airlines been given too much leeway in postponing necessary repairs?

Delta Airlines also came under fire. If early warning signs had been present, why hadn't the airline grounded the aircraft for a full inspection? Had corporate pressures for on-time departures and financial considerations taken precedence over safety? Families of the victims demanded accountability, filing lawsuits against Delta, the aircraft manufacturer, and even the regulatory agencies that had signed off on the aircraft's continued operation.

As hearings were scheduled and public pressure mounted, the overwhelming conclusion among aviation experts was clear: Delta Flight 1873's crash was preventable. If proper maintenance protocols had been followed, if hydraulic issues had been taken seriously, if stricter oversight had been in place, 187 lives could have been saved. The tragedy was not just a failure of machinery—it was a failure of systems, regulations, and priorities.

The final report was still months away, but the conversation had already shifted toward reforms, accountability, and ensuring that such a disaster never happened again. The crash of Delta Flight 1873 would not just be remembered as an accident—it would be remembered as a preventable catastrophe that exposed deep flaws in the aviation industry.

Chapter 6
Inside Delta Airlines

As news of the Delta Flight 1873 tragedy spread across the world, a somber mood settled over Delta Airlines' headquarters in Atlanta, Georgia. Executives, flight safety officials, and public relations teams scrambled to respond. The airline, one of the most respected in the industry, now found itself in the harsh spotlight of scrutiny. Inside the company's walls, meetings stretched late into the night, with leadership preparing for the inevitable barrage of media inquiries, regulatory investigations, and legal consequences.

In the hours following the crash, Delta's Crisis Management Team convened in the airline's emergency operations center. The CEO, safety directors, and legal counsel worked together to assess what was known. Their immediate priority was supporting the families of the victims, ensuring that every affected loved one received personal outreach, travel arrangements, and grief counseling. Delta quickly set up a family assistance center, a standard protocol in aviation disasters, providing families with private updates before the media.

At the same time, the airline's flight operations and maintenance teams were under immense pressure. Investigators from the National Transportation Safety Board (NTSB) had already requested maintenance logs, pilot training records, and recent aircraft inspections. Delta's engineers and technicians combed through the data, hoping to determine whether a mechanical failure had played a role. Every detail—from the aircraft's last checkup to reports of past technical issues—was scrutinized.

Meanwhile, Delta's public relations team faced an equally difficult challenge. Within hours, news headlines were unforgiving:

- *"Delta Flight 1873: What Went Wrong?"*
- *"Passengers Had No Chance—Airline Under Fire"*
- *"Could This Tragedy Have Been Prevented?"*

Social media erupted with speculation, and aviation analysts dissected every known fact on live television. Stock prices dipped, and Delta executives knew their response in the coming days could make or break public trust.

Internally, pilots and crew members across Delta's fleet felt the impact of the disaster. Flight attendants fielded nervous questions from passengers, while pilots reassured travelers of the airline's safety protocols. Employees grieved for their fallen colleagues, some of whom had trained alongside Captain Mark Reynolds and First Officer Jason Keller.

As the NTSB investigation unfolded, Delta faced a defining moment. Would this be a wake-up call for systemic change, or would the airline become another corporation bogged down in legal battles and public distrust? The next steps would determine whether Delta Airlines could weather the storm—or whether the fallout from Flight 1873 would leave a permanent scar on its reputation.

A History of Safety and Trust

Delta Airlines had long been recognized as one of the most reliable carriers in the aviation industry. With a strong safety record, rigorous pilot training programs, and advanced aircraft maintenance protocols, the airline had built a reputation that passengers trusted. For decades, Delta had been a leader in operational efficiency, ensuring that its fleet met the highest industry standards while maintaining a commitment to passenger safety.

The airline's history was marked by innovations in safety procedures, investments in fleet modernization, and a culture that prioritized pilot and crew preparedness. From its early days as a regional carrier to becoming one of the world's largest airlines, Delta had been known for strict maintenance policies and adherence to Federal Aviation Administration (FAA) regulations. Incidents and accidents were rare, and when they did occur, the airline worked closely with investigators to implement improvements and prevent future issues.

Delta's pilots and crew underwent extensive training, with simulations designed to prepare them for nearly every possible emergency scenario. Captain Mark Reynolds and First Officer Jason Keller had been among the best, both highly trained and experienced, having logged thousands of flight hours. Their ability to respond professionally under pressure had been evident in the final moments of Delta Flight 1873, where they had exhausted every possible maneuver in their attempt to regain control.

Aircraft maintenance had also been a key pillar of the airline's safety strategy. Delta maintained one of the largest and most sophisticated maintenance, repair, and overhaul (MRO) facilities in the world, ensuring that its fleet remained in top condition. Routine checks, in-depth inspections, and system diagnostics were part of daily operations, making the sudden hydraulic failure of Flight 1873 all the more shocking. The airline had historically been proactive in grounding aircraft with unresolved maintenance issues, which made the decision to allow this plane to continue flying despite previous hydraulic warnings a troubling deviation from standard policy.

For decades, passengers had trusted Delta, believing in its commitment to safety and reliability. Frequent flyers felt secure in the airline's ability to maintain aircraft and train pilots to handle emergencies. The company had been among the first to adopt cutting-edge technology in predictive maintenance, flight data monitoring, and crisis response strategies, all aimed at preventing incidents before they could escalate into disasters.

This reputation made the crash of Flight 1873 even more devastating. It was not just a tragedy in itself—it was a rupture in the trust that millions of passengers had placed in the airline. How had an airline with such a solid record allowed an aircraft with a known mechanical issue to remain in operation? How had a system designed to prevent failures let this one slip through? The answers to these questions would shape the conversation around airline safety, regulatory oversight, and corporate responsibility in the months that followed.

The loss of Flight 1873 would become a defining moment, not just for Delta, but for the entire aviation industry. In the past, the airline had emerged from challenges with a renewed commitment to safety and improvement. Now, as it faced the scrutiny of grieving families, government regulators, and the public, it had to confront the reality that even a legacy of trust and safety could be shaken in an instant. The future of airline safety would depend on how Delta and the industry responded to this tragedy, ensuring that the lessons of Flight 1873 were not forgotten.

Internal Reactions to the Tragedy

Inside Delta Airlines' corporate headquarters, the crash of Flight 1873 sent shockwaves through every department. The news broke fast, and before executives could even fully process what had happened, the world was already demanding answers. The airline's crisis response team was immediately activated, scrambling to contain the fallout, communicate with authorities, and prepare for what would become one of the biggest public relations challenges in the company's history.

At the highest levels of the organization, executives faced an impossible situation. Delta had long prided itself on safety and operational excellence, but now it was at the center of an aviation disaster that had claimed 187 lives. The CEO called an emergency meeting, bringing together legal teams, public relations specialists, safety officers, and operational managers to assess the situation and plan the next steps.

The first priority was communication. The airline had to contact the families of the victims, an agonizing task that would set the tone for how the public viewed Delta's response. A team of specially trained representatives was dispatched to airports and hotels where families were waiting, offering support, information, and grief counseling. At the same time, call centers were overwhelmed with frantic relatives seeking confirmation of their worst fears. Some family members received the heartbreaking news over the phone, while others learned of the crash through news reports before Delta could reach them.

Internally, employees were reeling. Flight crews, mechanics, and customer service agents—people who had dedicated their careers to ensuring passengers arrived safely at their destinations—were struggling to come to terms with the loss. Some had personally known the pilots, flight attendants, or frequent passengers on board. Many felt a deep sense of guilt, wondering if something had been missed. Mechanics who had worked on the aircraft prior to the flight were questioned and put on administrative leave while the investigation continued. The weight of the tragedy hung heavily over everyone.

In the operations and safety division, investigators were pouring over maintenance logs, pilot schedules, and aircraft diagnostics to understand how this could have happened. Engineers reviewed past reports of hydraulic issues, trying to determine whether there had been warning signs that were ignored or misjudged. The revelation that previous maintenance concerns about the hydraulic system had been deferred was deeply unsettling, fueling speculation that corporate decisions about cost-cutting and efficiency may have played a role in the tragedy.

The public relations team was in full crisis mode, crafting official statements while trying to contain the growing media storm. The first press conference was tense, with journalists pressing Delta executives for explanations they didn't yet have. The CEO expressed deep condolences, vowing full cooperation with investigators and immediate safety reviews. But for many watching, words were not enough.

As days passed, internal tensions rose. Employees at all levels were feeling the pressure, from customer service agents receiving angry calls to executives facing scrutiny from lawmakers and regulators. The board of directors convened behind closed doors, discussing damage control strategies, legal liabilities, and whether resignations would be necessary to restore public trust.

Inside Delta's corporate offices, the once steady foundation of confidence and pride in safety had been shaken to its core. The airline was facing its greatest crisis yet, and how it responded in the coming weeks would determine whether it could recover—or if the legacy of Flight 1873 would forever define its future.

Crisis Management in the Spotlight

Delta Airlines found itself in the center of an international crisis following the crash of Flight 1873. The company, known for its rigorous safety record and operational excellence, was now under intense scrutiny from the public, regulators, the media, and grieving families. How the airline handled the aftermath would shape not only its reputation but also the broader conversation around corporate accountability in aviation disasters.

The immediate priority was managing communication. Delta's crisis response team worked around the clock, crafting public statements, coordinating with investigators, and preparing spokespersons for the onslaught of media inquiries. The first press conference came within hours of the crash, with Delta's CEO standing before cameras, expressing condolences and promising full cooperation with authorities. But the lack of concrete answers only fueled more questions. Journalists pressed for details on maintenance records, pilot error possibilities, and mechanical failures, while airline representatives carefully walked the line between transparency and legal risk.

Internally, the crisis response was chaotic. Executives and legal teams scrambled to control the narrative, while employees across the organization felt the weight of the disaster. Flight attendants, pilots, and customer service staff—many of whom had nothing to do with the tragedy—were facing the public's anger firsthand. Call centers were overwhelmed with furious and heartbroken family members, demanding explanations and accountability. Some social media accounts were flooded with messages of outrage, while others pleaded for updates on survivors.

Delta's legal team worked aggressively to prepare for potential lawsuits. Families of victims were already coming together to demand justice, and legal experts predicted multi-million-dollar claims against the airline. The airline had to strike a balance between offering support to grieving families and protecting itself from litigation. Compensation funds were quickly established, and grief counseling services were offered, but for many, these efforts felt hollow in the face of such devastating loss.

Social media played a massive role in amplifying the crisis, turning it into a public relations nightmare. Hashtags like #Delta1873, #AccountabilityFor187, and #NeverAgain trended worldwide, with passengers sharing their own concerns about airline safety and maintenance practices. Delta's crisis communication team attempted to control the online conversation, issuing carefully worded updates and responding to public concerns, but once trust was broken, it became nearly impossible to rebuild overnight.

Behind closed doors, Delta's board of directors and senior executives debated how to proceed. Some pushed for immediate resignations at the highest levels to show accountability, while others argued that stability was needed to lead the company through the storm. The CEO, now under immense pressure, faced calls to step down, as public perception turned against airline leadership. Meanwhile, shareholders were growing restless, watching Delta's stock price plummet in the wake of the disaster.

At the same time, Delta was facing regulatory scrutiny from the Federal Aviation Administration (FAA), the National Transportation Safety Board (NTSB), and Congress. Investigators were already uncovering troubling maintenance records, raising questions about whether corporate cost-cutting measures had played a role in the aircraft's hydraulic system failure. Lawmakers announced hearings to examine safety regulations, airline oversight, and potential systemic failures that allowed a plane with prior warnings to keep flying.

The pressure to act was immediate. Delta announced sweeping internal safety audits, grounding similar aircraft for inspection and pledging new investments in maintenance and training. The airline also promised full cooperation with investigators, hoping to rebuild trust before irreversible damage was done.

In the world of aviation, how an airline handles a crisis can define its legacy. The crash of Flight 1873 had already shattered lives, but the response in the days, weeks, and months that followed would determine whether Delta Airlines could recover—or whether this tragedy would permanently tarnish its name.

The Public Relations Nightmare

Delta Airlines was in freefall, not just in the skies but in the court of public opinion. The crash of Flight 1873 had already shattered lives, but now the airline was facing a different kind of disaster—one unfolding in the media, in boardrooms, and across social platforms. What began as a tragic accident had turned into a full-blown public relations nightmare, with Delta's reputation on the line and the world demanding answers.

The first press conference should have been an opportunity for the airline to show leadership, accountability, and compassion, but it quickly spiraled out of control. Delta's CEO, flanked by legal and communications advisors, opened with a statement expressing deep sorrow for the loss of life and a commitment to cooperating with investigators. But when journalists pressed for details on prior maintenance concerns, possible negligence, and the pilots' last moments, the responses were vague, rehearsed, and evasive. The lack of concrete answers only fueled public suspicion.

Social media erupted within minutes. Hashtags like #Delta1873, #JusticeFor187, and #CorporateNegligence trended worldwide, amplifying the anger of grieving families and outraged passengers. Leaked maintenance records began circulating online, showing that prior hydraulic issues had been reported on the aircraft but marked as "non-critical" and deferred for future inspections. Aviation analysts, independent journalists, and even former Delta employees took to Twitter, Instagram, and TikTok to break down the red flags, further eroding public trust.

Delta's social media response team was overwhelmed. Carefully crafted corporate statements were drowned out by thousands of furious comments demanding transparency. Every post the airline made—whether about refunds, condolences, or unrelated travel updates—was flooded with accusations of negligence and greed. Videos from passengers who had flown on the same aircraft before the crash, describing strange noises and past delays, gained millions of views.

Family members of the victims became the face of public outrage, giving emotional interviews on national television, sharing heartbreaking stories of lost loved ones. Some showed screenshots of unanswered emails and delayed responses from Delta, while others accused the airline of stonewalling them in their search for information. Lawsuits were already being filed, and each new revelation only intensified the PR disaster.

In response to the growing backlash, Delta's leadership attempted to shift gears. The company grounded similar aircraft, announced a full-scale safety review, and pledged millions in compensation to the victims' families. They brought in crisis management experts, hired high-profile lawyers, and launched damage-control marketing campaigns emphasizing their history of safety and commitment to change. But it was too little, too late.

News outlets continued to dig, uncovering internal memos showing that financial concerns had influenced past maintenance decisions. Public trust in the airline industry as a whole began to waver, and calls for stricter regulations grew louder. Lawmakers seized the moment, demanding hearings on aviation safety standards and corporate accountability.

Stockholders were watching, and Delta's market value began to plummet. Investors worried that legal settlements, government fines, and a tarnished reputation would cripple the airline for years. Behind closed doors, board members debated whether top executives, including the CEO, should resign in an effort to show accountability.

The public relations nightmare was far from over. The crash of Flight 1873 had already cemented itself as one of the most tragic aviation disasters in recent history, but now it was a symbol of corporate failure, regulatory lapses, and the human cost of overlooked warnings. The question was no longer just what had gone wrong, but whether Delta Airlines could ever recover from it.

Chapter 7
The Families' Fight for Truth

The first 24 hours after the crash of Delta Flight 1873 were filled with shock, grief, and disbelief. As news of the tragedy spread, families of the passengers desperately tried to get information. Many had last spoken to their loved ones just hours before takeoff, unaware that it would be their final conversation. Now, they were left with nothing but uncertainty and pain.

Delta Airlines, following aviation disaster protocol, had already set up a Family Assistance Center, where grieving relatives were directed for information and support. Company representatives offered condolences, grief counselors were made available, and travel accommodations were provided for those who needed to reach the crash site. But no words, no corporate statements, and no carefully worded apologies could fill the void left by their loss.

In the days that followed, grief turned into a demand for answers. Families began asking the same painful questions:

- What went wrong?
- Could this have been prevented?
- Who is responsible for this tragedy?

As details of the crash investigation unfolded, frustrations grew. The National Transportation Safety Board (NTSB) had secured the black boxes, but analyzing the data would take time. The cause of the crash remained unknown, and for the families, every passing day without clarity felt like an eternity.

Many relatives joined forces, forming victims' advocacy groups to push for transparency. Some hired legal teams, preparing to hold Delta Airlines, the aircraft manufacturer, and any responsible party accountable. Press conferences were held, where emotional pleas were made for full disclosure of the investigation findings. Families demanded that this not become another unsolved aviation disaster lost in bureaucratic red tape.

Lawyers representing the families began filing wrongful death lawsuits, alleging negligence on the part of Delta Airlines, its maintenance teams, and potentially even the aircraft's manufacturer. Had the plane been properly inspected? Had known issues been ignored? These were the questions they wanted answered—not just for justice, but to prevent another tragedy.

As months passed, families found themselves navigating a system filled with corporate defenses, government investigations, and complex legal battles. Some sought new safety regulations, advocating for stricter airline maintenance requirements and better pilot training programs. Others simply wanted closure.

But one thing was clear: they would not let the story of Delta Flight 1873 fade away. For them, this was more than just an aviation disaster—it was a fight for truth, justice, and change.

The Grief of Lost Loved Ones

The grief that followed the crash of Delta Flight 1873 was immeasurable. The sudden, violent loss of 187 lives left families, friends, and entire communities shattered. What had begun as an ordinary flight had ended in unthinkable devastation, and for those left behind, there was no way to prepare for the pain that followed.

For the families of the victims, the nightmare began the moment they heard the news. Some were waiting at the airport, watching in confusion as the arrival board changed from "On Time" to "Cancelled", their worst fears forming before they were confirmed. Others received phone calls—some from Delta representatives, some from news alerts before the airline could even reach them. The pain of losing someone is unbearable under any circumstances, but the sudden, public nature of this disaster magnified the shock and agony.

At the designated family assistance centers, grief counselors and Delta representatives tried to offer support, but there was no comfort in words. Mothers collapsed, fathers held back tears, siblings stared in stunned silence, unable to accept what had happened. Many clung to the hope that their loved one had somehow survived, desperately asking for names of passengers pulled from the wreckage, only to be met with grim expressions and quiet shakes of the head.

Some families learned of the crash through news reports before Delta even contacted them. A wife waiting for her husband to return from a business trip saw the burning wreckage on television, knowing that her world had just changed forever. A teenage girl, excitedly texting her mother about her arrival, was met with radio silence before seeing the headlines flash across her phone screen. The cruel speed at which the world learned about the crash contrasted painfully with the slow, agonizing process of receiving official confirmation.

For those who lost entire families, the weight of grief was unbearable. One father had put his wife and two young children on Flight 1873, planning to join them the following day. Now, his entire world had been taken from him in an instant. Another couple, newly engaged, had been traveling to celebrate their wedding plans, a future that would now never come.

Funerals took place across the country, each one a stark reminder of how many lives had been lost. The victims were mothers, fathers, children, friends, students, workers, dreamers—people who had boarded the plane expecting to arrive safely, only to become part of a tragedy that should never have happened. The sheer scale of loss was overwhelming.

For many, the grief quickly turned into anger. As news emerged that maintenance issues had been flagged but not addressed, families felt betrayed. Their loved ones had not just been lost in an accident; they had been victims of systemic failures, ignored warnings, and possible negligence. The pain of knowing that this might have been preventable only deepened the suffering.

Memorials were erected in the cities where the victims had lived, at the airports they had departed from, and even at the crash site itself. Candlelight vigils drew thousands of mourners, strangers coming together to honor those lost and demand accountability. Loved ones left behind letters, flowers, and photographs, trying in some way to hold on to the people they had lost.

Time moved forward, but for those grieving, the loss remained frozen in place. Every missed birthday, every empty chair at the dinner table, every holiday spent in silence was a reminder of what had been taken from them. No investigation, no compensation, no public apology would ever bring back what had been lost.

The grief of lost loved ones did not fade—it simply became something they carried, forever intertwined with the memory of Flight 1873.

Demands for Justice and Accountability

In the wake of the Delta Flight 1873 tragedy, grief quickly turned into outrage. Families of the victims, aviation safety advocates, and the general public demanded answers, accountability, and justice for the 187 lives lost. As the investigation uncovered troubling details about prior warnings, deferred maintenance, and regulatory lapses, it became clear that this was not just an accident—it was a preventable catastrophe that had cost innocent lives.

Families of the victims were the first to demand justice. Many had initially been in shock, struggling to process the loss of their loved ones, but as details emerged about the aircraft's history of hydraulic failures, their grief turned to anger. They wanted to know why a plane with prior warnings of mechanical issues had been allowed to fly, why maintenance concerns had been ignored, and why their loved ones had to pay the ultimate price for corporate decisions.

Legal teams quickly mobilized, and within days, multiple lawsuits were filed against Delta Airlines, the aircraft manufacturer, and even the Federal Aviation Administration (FAA). Plaintiffs accused the airline of negligence, claiming that it had prior knowledge of hydraulic system defects and still chose to keep the aircraft in service. Attorneys representing the victims' families called for multi-million-dollar settlements, not just as compensation, but as a statement that airlines could not put profits over passenger safety.

As public pressure mounted, Congress called for hearings on aviation safety, summoning Delta executives, FAA officials, and aviation regulators to testify under oath. Lawmakers wanted to know if systemic failures in airline safety regulations had contributed to the crash. Investigators revealed that several prior hydraulic failures had been flagged on Delta's fleet but had been marked as non-critical or deferred for later inspections. The hearings became a televised spectacle, with grieving family members sitting in the audience, their presence a powerful reminder of the human cost of regulatory failures.

The FAA itself came under intense scrutiny, as evidence suggested that it had signed off on maintenance deferrals without fully investigating the risks. Critics accused the agency of being too lenient with major airlines, allowing them to prioritize cost efficiency over immediate safety concerns. Some lawmakers called for a complete overhaul of FAA oversight policies, demanding stricter enforcement of safety regulations and harsher penalties for airlines that ignored maintenance red flags.

Aviation unions also joined the fight, with pilots, flight attendants, and maintenance workers speaking out about the corporate culture of cost-cutting. Some Delta mechanics came forward anonymously, claiming that they had been pressured to downplay or delay repairs to keep aircraft in service. A former Delta pilot testified that pilots had reported irregular hydraulic pressure on certain aircraft before, but those concerns were often dismissed as routine wear and tear.

The public, too, played a crucial role in the demands for justice. Social media campaigns kept the pressure on Delta, the FAA, and policymakers, ensuring that the tragedy was not forgotten. Hashtags like #JusticeFor187 and #NeverAgain trended for weeks, with people sharing stories of other near-misses, maintenance concerns, and fears about airline safety practices.

Delta, now facing a major crisis of trust, tried to get ahead of the outrage by announcing new safety measures, including an internal audit of maintenance procedures, mandatory retraining for mechanics, and stricter compliance policies. The airline also set up a fund for victims' families, but many saw it as a damage control move rather than a true commitment to accountability.

For the families, none of it was enough. They wanted real change, not just policy adjustments and settlements. They wanted individuals held responsible, whether it was executives who had signed off on delayed maintenance, FAA officials who had failed in oversight, or airline leaders who had prioritized revenue over safety.

As investigations continued and legal battles escalated, one thing was certain—this was not just about Delta Flight 1873 anymore. It was about changing an industry, ensuring that no other families would have to suffer the way these 187 families had. The tragedy had exposed deep flaws in aviation safety oversight, and now, those demanding justice were determined to make sure that those responsible were held accountable, and that real reform followed.

Legal Battles Begin

The legal battles surrounding Delta Flight 1873 began almost immediately after the tragedy, as grieving families, aviation experts, and regulatory bodies sought answers, accountability, and justice. What had initially been framed as a mechanical failure was quickly revealing itself to be a case of negligence, oversight failures, and corporate cost-cutting that had placed passengers' lives at risk. The question was no longer just what happened—it was who was responsible and how they would be held accountable.

Within days of the crash, lawsuits were filed against Delta Airlines, the aircraft manufacturer, and even the Federal Aviation Administration (FAA). The families of the victims, represented by some of the country's top aviation attorneys, accused the airline of negligence, claiming that it had prior knowledge of hydraulic system defects and still chose to keep the aircraft in service. Attorneys argued that if Delta had properly addressed maintenance concerns, the catastrophic failure could have been prevented. The lawsuits sought compensation for wrongful death, emotional distress, and punitive damages, with some estimates placing total liability in the hundreds of millions of dollars.

Delta's legal team quickly moved into defense mode, hiring high-profile lawyers to protect the airline's interests. In public statements, the company expressed deep sorrow for the tragedy but denied any intentional wrongdoing. Delta's attorneys argued that the airline had followed all required FAA safety regulations, deferring maintenance in accordance with industry standards. However, as internal documents surfaced, revealing that multiple reports of hydraulic failures had been flagged on the aircraft but deferred for future inspections, the airline found itself in an increasingly defensible position.

The FAA also faced legal action, as families and advocacy groups accused the agency of failing to enforce strict safety protocols. Lawyers argued that the FAA had become too lenient with major airlines, allowing self-reporting and deferred maintenance decisions that prioritized cost efficiency over safety. Some legal experts even suggested that the agency's close ties with the airline industry had contributed to a culture of regulatory complacency that had played a role in the tragedy.

The aircraft manufacturer was also dragged into the legal fight. Investigators had uncovered stress fractures in a key hydraulic line, suggesting a potential design flaw that had made the aircraft vulnerable to catastrophic failure. Plaintiffs argued that the manufacturer had either failed to recognize the flaw during production or had downplayed the risks associated with aging hydraulic components.

As lawsuits piled up, Congressional hearings were scheduled, bringing Delta executives, FAA officials, and aviation engineers before lawmakers to testify under oath. The hearings quickly became a media spectacle, with grieving family members sitting in the audience as executives struggled to explain why a plane with prior hydraulic warnings was allowed to fly. Legislators pressed Delta's leadership on whether financial considerations had influenced maintenance decisions, and whether mechanics had been pressured to approve aircraft that weren't fully operational.

Meanwhile, class-action lawsuits were being prepared by passengers who had narrowly missed being on Flight 1873. Frequent Delta travelers and other airline customers began to demand full transparency on maintenance policies, questioning whether other aircraft had similar deferred maintenance issues.

Insurance companies were also caught in the legal storm. Delta's insurers faced massive payout claims, and negotiations over settlements and liability limits turned into a battle of their own. The airline sought to cap liability payouts, while families and legal teams pushed for maximum compensation to reflect the magnitude of the loss.

As months passed, some settlements were reached, but many families refused to settle, pushing for full trials to expose what they believed was corporate negligence and regulatory failure. The legal war over Flight 1873 had just begun, and its outcome would not only determine who would be held responsible for the tragedy but also set a precedent for airline safety standards, corporate liability, and regulatory oversight for years to come.

The Power of Collective Action

In the aftermath of the Delta Flight 1873 tragedy, grief-stricken families, aviation safety advocates, and outraged citizens came together to demand justice, accountability, and reform. What started as individual pain and loss soon transformed into a collective movement, driven by the conviction that this tragedy could not be allowed to happen again. The power of collective action became a force that airlines, regulators, and lawmakers could no longer ignore.

The families of the victims were the first to mobilize. Initially consumed by grief, many found strength in unity, forming support groups and online forums to share their stories and experiences. Parents who had lost children, spouses who had lost their partners, and children who had lost their parents came together, united by a singular mission: to hold those responsible accountable and to ensure airline safety was never taken for granted again.

Public vigils and rallies were organized across the country, drawing thousands of supporters. Candles were lit outside Delta's headquarters, FAA offices, and even the steps of Congress as people demanded answers and action. What had begun as isolated lawsuits quickly evolved into a nationwide call for reform, with families leading the charge in demanding stricter airline maintenance policies, more rigorous FAA oversight, and harsher penalties for negligence in the aviation industry.

Social media became a powerful tool for spreading awareness. The hashtags #JusticeFor187, #NeverAgain, and #Delta1873 trended for weeks, amplifying the voices of victims' families and putting immense pressure on Delta Airlines, government officials, and regulatory bodies. Survivors and family members of past aviation disasters joined the conversation, offering support and calling for long-overdue changes in aviation safety protocols.

Legal action was another crucial avenue of collective strength. Class-action lawsuits gained momentum, with families refusing to settle quietly. Instead, they pushed for full transparency, demanding that internal communications, maintenance records, and corporate decision-making processes be made public. Lawyers representing the families worked together, forming a unified front against Delta, the aircraft manufacturer, and the FAA. The goal was not just financial compensation—it was systemic change.

The movement soon gained the attention of lawmakers, many of whom were already facing public pressure to address aviation safety failures. Congress was flooded with letters, petitions, and calls demanding reform in how airlines handled safety concerns, how the FAA monitored airline compliance, and how much influence corporate interests had in regulatory decisions. Lawmakers could no longer ignore the mounting pressure, and bipartisan committees were formed to investigate the failures that led to the crash.

A major victory came when Congress announced a sweeping aviation safety reform bill, aimed at eliminating deferred maintenance loopholes, enforcing stricter reporting guidelines, and increasing penalties for airlines that failed to prioritize passenger safety. The bill was a direct result of collective action, proving that when families, advocates, and the public stood together, change was possible.

The fight was not over, but the families of Flight 1873 had transformed their pain into power. What had once been a senseless tragedy had now sparked a movement for justice, accountability, and reform. Through collective action, they ensured that their loved ones were not just statistics in an aviation disaster—they were the reason the world would never turn a blind eye to airline safety again.

Chapter 8
Unraveling the Technical Causes

As investigators sifted through the wreckage of Delta Flight 1873, their primary focus was on determining the exact cause of the disaster. Was it a mechanical failure, human error, or a combination of factors? The National Transportation Safety Board (NTSB), alongside engineers from the Federal Aviation Administration (FAA) and aviation experts from Delta Airlines, worked tirelessly to reconstruct the final moments of the flight.

The first breakthrough came when forensic teams recovered the flight data recorder (FDR) and cockpit voice recorder (CVR). The black boxes held the key to what went wrong in the aircraft's last minutes. Analysts immediately began decoding the flight path, control inputs, engine performance, and onboard system readings. Meanwhile, the cockpit voice recorder revealed the pilots' final conversations—every command, every warning, and every attempt to regain control.

As the data was analyzed, a troubling pattern emerged. Initial findings pointed to a mechanical anomaly within the aircraft's hydraulic control system, which plays a crucial role in stabilizing the plane during flight. Reports suggested that a sudden loss of hydraulic pressure had affected the aircraft's ability to respond to pilot inputs, making it nearly impossible to correct the descent.

Further investigation into the wreckage confirmed severe damage to the left-side hydraulic actuator, a critical component controlling the aircraft's ailerons and flaps. Metallurgical analysis showed signs of stress fractures and fatigue, raising questions about whether a pre-existing flaw had been overlooked during routine maintenance checks.

However, mechanical failure alone did not fully explain the tragedy. The NTSB team also examined the aircraft's maintenance history, looking for delayed repairs, past reported malfunctions, and any records of hydraulic issues. A chilling discovery revealed that similar failures had been flagged in previous flights, but they had not been deemed severe enough to ground the plane.

Additionally, experts explored the possibility of sensor malfunctions or avionics failures, which might have provided incorrect data to the pilots, leading them to make incorrect adjustments in the crucial moments before impact. The aircraft's autopilot system was also scrutinized, as preliminary reports suggested that it had disengaged suddenly, leaving the pilots to manually control an unstable aircraft.

As these revelations surfaced, public scrutiny intensified. Families of the victims demanded to know why these mechanical warnings were ignored and whether this tragedy could have been prevented through stricter maintenance protocols. The airline industry braced for the impact of the investigation's findings, knowing that the results could lead to new safety regulations and legal consequences.

While the final NTSB report was still months away, one thing was becoming clear—Delta Flight 1873 was not just an accident. It was the result of a system that had failed at multiple levels.

The Aircraft's Maintenance History

As investigators delved into the maintenance records of the ill-fated Delta Flight 1873, a troubling pattern began to emerge. The aircraft, a widely used commercial jet, had undergone routine inspections and servicing, but hidden beneath the layers of paperwork were red flags that had been overlooked, deferred, or dismissed as non-critical issues. What at first appeared to be an unavoidable mechanical failure was increasingly looking like a preventable disaster caused by missed opportunities, cost-cutting, and regulatory gaps.

The National Transportation Safety Board (NTSB), in collaboration with the Federal Aviation Administration (FAA) and independent aviation experts, began to piece together the full maintenance history of the aircraft. What they found was deeply unsettling. Over the previous six months, maintenance logs had recorded multiple reports of fluctuating hydraulic pressure levels, particularly affecting one of the primary hydraulic systems responsible for controlling the aircraft's rudders, ailerons, and landing gear. These anomalies had been documented by pilots and mechanics, but instead of triggering immediate repairs, they had been marked as "non-critical" and placed on a deferred maintenance schedule.

The deferral system, which allows airlines to postpone certain repairs deemed non-urgent, was designed to balance operational efficiency with safety. However, in this case, investigators questioned whether the airline had relied too heavily on deferrals to keep the aircraft flying, rather than grounding it for a full inspection and repair. The logs revealed that, on at least three separate occasions, pilots had reported difficulty in maintaining hydraulic pressure mid-flight, yet each time, the aircraft had been cleared to continue operations.

Further analysis uncovered a particularly alarming entry from three months before the crash. A maintenance technician had documented a sudden and unexplained drop in hydraulic pressure during a routine check, recommending that the system be monitored closely. However, rather than conducting an immediate deep-dive inspection, the recommendation was overruled by supervisors, and the aircraft continued flying without major intervention. This decision, investigators suggested, may have sealed the fate of Flight 1873.

As the investigation deepened, attention turned toward corporate decision-making and maintenance budgeting. Delta Airlines, like all major carriers, had strict cost-control measures, ensuring that planes remained in service for as long as possible without unnecessary disruptions. Interviews with former and current airline mechanics suggested a culture in which delaying repairs to maintain flight schedules was not uncommon. Some employees, speaking anonymously, admitted feeling pressured to sign off on aircraft deemed airworthy, even when concerns lingered about long-term wear and tear on critical systems.

A closer look at manufacturer bulletins and industry-wide maintenance recommendations revealed that similar hydraulic failures had occurred in other aircraft of the same model, though none had led to such a catastrophic outcome. Several other airlines had flagged hydraulic system vulnerabilities and opted for early replacements of aging components, but Delta had continued operating the aircraft under standard FAA guidelines, which did not require immediate corrective action.

Regulators now faced a difficult question: Had existing aviation safety policies been too lenient, allowing airlines to prioritize cost efficiency over passenger safety? The fact that FAA inspectors had reviewed and approved the deferred maintenance schedules suggested that oversight agencies had either failed to recognize the risks or had been too accommodating toward airline industry interests.

As details of the maintenance history emerged, public outrage grew. Families of the victims were horrified to learn that warning signs had been present for months but had not been acted upon. The idea that their loved ones had died not due to an unpredictable accident, but because of avoidable negligence, fueled lawsuits, congressional hearings, and calls for sweeping industry reforms.

Ultimately, the aircraft's maintenance history became a key piece of evidence in the legal and regulatory battles that followed. The question was no longer just what had gone wrong, but why those responsible had failed to prevent it—and how the airline industry would be forced to change as a result.

Design Flaws and Possible Malfunctions

As investigators scrutinized the wreckage of Delta Flight 1873, they focused on whether the disaster had been caused solely by maintenance failures or if deeper design flaws in the aircraft's systems had contributed to the catastrophe. While the airline's deferral of maintenance was a critical factor, evidence pointed to potential vulnerabilities in the hydraulic system's design—flaws that, under the right conditions, could have made a mechanical failure not just possible, but inevitable.

One of the most alarming findings was the simultaneous failure of all three hydraulic systems, an event that should have been virtually impossible. Commercial aircraft are designed with redundant hydraulic systems to ensure that if one fails, the others can compensate. Yet, in the case of Flight 1873, the failure spread rapidly across all three systems, leaving the pilots with almost no control over the aircraft. Investigators suspected that a single-point vulnerability—a flaw in the design where one failure could cascade through the entire system—was to blame.

The flight data recorder (FDR) revealed that the aircraft's hydraulic pressure began fluctuating approximately 15 minutes before the mayday call, meaning the failure was progressive rather than instantaneous. The NTSB worked with aerospace engineers to analyze whether the aircraft's hydraulic lines had been designed in a way that made them prone to rapid pressure loss. One troubling theory suggested that the routing of hydraulic lines too close to high-temperature components may have weakened the system over time.

Another key discovery came when metallurgical experts examined fragments of the ruptured hydraulic lines recovered from the crash site. The analysis found evidence of microcracks and stress fractures, signs that long-term wear and metal fatigue may have played a role in the failure. These microcracks were consistent with known weaknesses in high-pressure hydraulic tubing, a problem that had been observed in earlier models of the same aircraft. Some airlines had proactively reinforced or replaced these components, but Flight 1873's aircraft had continued operating under standard guidelines.

Further investigations revealed that the hydraulic backup systems may not have functioned as designed. Modern aircraft include backup electrical and mechanical systems intended to provide some degree of control even in the event of complete hydraulic failure. However, cockpit voice recordings and data from the FDR indicated that the pilots' manual override attempts had little to no effect, suggesting that the aircraft's backup systems were either compromised or inadequate for the severity of the failure.

Investigators also reviewed manufacturer documentation and past service bulletins, looking for any history of design modifications or safety recommendations related to the hydraulic system. Alarmingly, previous airworthiness directives had been issued for similar models, warning airlines to closely inspect high-pressure hydraulic tubing for premature wear and potential rupture risks. While no direct order had been given to replace components, multiple airlines had taken proactive steps to reinforce their aircraft's hydraulic integrity. Delta, however, had followed minimum regulatory requirements, which did not mandate immediate corrective action.

As these findings emerged, the aircraft manufacturer faced intense scrutiny. Critics argued that known vulnerabilities in the hydraulic system should have been addressed through a mandatory redesign, rather than relying on airlines to implement optional modifications. Some aviation engineers speculated that the failure could have been prevented with better shielding of hydraulic components, improved redundancy in fluid routing, or more rigorous pressure monitoring systems.

The combination of aging materials, design vulnerabilities, and an over-reliance on deferred maintenance created a perfect storm that led to Flight 1873's loss of control. The tragedy exposed not just one flaw, but multiple weak points—some in the aircraft's design, some in airline maintenance culture, and others in the regulatory framework that allowed these risks to persist.

With lawsuits mounting and public pressure intensifying, both Delta and the aircraft manufacturer faced tough questions about how much they knew, when they knew it, and why no action had been taken before disaster struck. The findings reinforced a chilling reality: Flight 1873 may not have been an anomaly, but the result of flaws that could threaten other aircraft still in service.

Expert Analyses and Disagreements

As the investigation into Delta Flight 1873 progressed, aviation experts, engineers, and regulatory officials engaged in heated debates over what had truly caused the disaster. While many agreed that hydraulic failure played a major role, there was no single consensus on whether it was a result of deferred maintenance, a fundamental design flaw, pilot error, or a combination of all three. The divide between industry professionals, government regulators, and independent experts led to contradictory reports, conflicting testimonies, and a battle over accountability that further complicated the legal and public response.

The National Transportation Safety Board (NTSB), responsible for the official investigation, maintained that the primary cause of the crash was a catastrophic failure in the aircraft's hydraulic systems, made worse by pre-existing metal fatigue in critical components. Their findings pointed to stress fractures in the high-pressure hydraulic tubing, which had likely developed over time due to wear and exposure to extreme temperature fluctuations. This was backed by metallurgical analysis of the recovered wreckage, which showed that the hydraulic lines had weakened long before the final flight.

However, independent aerospace engineers pushed back against this explanation, arguing that hydraulic failures alone do not typically lead to a total loss of aircraft control. Some experts believed that the failure of backup systems, including electrical and mechanical redundancies, suggested a broader system-wide malfunction that had not been properly addressed in the NTSB's preliminary report. They questioned why manual override attempts by the pilots had seemingly no effect, implying that the aircraft's fail-safe systems had not functioned as designed.

One of the most controversial disputes emerged between the NTSB and the aircraft manufacturer, which argued that the plane's hydraulic design met all safety standards and had functioned correctly in thousands of flights before the crash. The manufacturer suggested that deferred maintenance and improper airline oversight, rather than any fundamental design flaw, had contributed to the hydraulic system's failure. They cited several airlines that had proactively reinforced their hydraulic lines without being required to do so and questioned why Delta had chosen not to implement additional protective measures despite warning signs from prior flights.

Delta Airlines, in its defense, pointed to FAA-approved maintenance protocols, arguing that it had followed standard industry procedures for addressing non-critical hydraulic concerns. Delta executives insisted that the airline had acted within regulatory guidelines, placing the burden of responsibility on manufacturers and oversight agencies for not issuing mandatory safety upgrades. They pushed back against claims that cost-cutting had influenced maintenance decisions, arguing that no regulatory body had warned them that the aircraft was unsafe to fly.

The Federal Aviation Administration (FAA) found itself in a difficult position, caught between public outrage, industry pressure, and legislative scrutiny. While acknowledging that Delta's maintenance deferrals had followed legal guidelines, FAA officials admitted that current regulations allowed airlines too much discretion in postponing repairs. The agency faced criticism for not enforcing stricter safety checks on aircraft with multiple recorded hydraulic anomalies, raising questions about whether the FAA had become too lenient in its oversight of major airlines.

Pilot unions and aviation safety advocates entered the debate, siding with the NTSB's findings but also emphasizing that design flaws played a larger role than initially acknowledged. They argued that the rapid progression of hydraulic failure across all three systems was highly unusual and suggested that the aircraft's control system had a critical vulnerability that needed to be addressed industry-wide. Some pilots expressed concerns that other aircraft in service could be at risk if similar vulnerabilities were present in their hydraulic designs.

The debate over pilot response also became a controversial point of contention. While cockpit voice recordings confirmed that Captain Mark Reynolds and First Officer Jason Keller had followed emergency protocols exactly, some critics speculated whether alternative techniques, such as adjusting engine thrust earlier in the failure, could have extended the pilots' control over the aircraft. However, most aviation professionals rejected the idea that pilot error had been a significant factor, emphasizing that the crew had been placed in an impossible situation with no viable recovery options.

As Congressional hearings and legal battles unfolded, the disagreements between experts, corporations, and regulators created a complex and polarizing landscape. Families of the victims, desperate for accountability, struggled to make sense of the conflicting narratives. Some sided with the belief that corporate negligence and deferred maintenance were to blame, while others believed a fundamental flaw in aircraft design had been ignored for years.

With lawsuits, legislative reforms, and industry-wide safety changes at stake, the battle over the true cause of Flight 1873's tragedy was far from over. The final investigative report would determine more than just the facts—it would shape the future of airline safety, regulatory policies, and corporate responsibility in aviation for years to come.

The Final Report

After months of intensive investigation, expert testimony, and public scrutiny, the National Transportation Safety Board (NTSB) released its final report on the crash of Delta Flight 1873. The report, spanning hundreds of pages, provided a comprehensive breakdown of the sequence of failures that led to the disaster. While the official findings did not provide absolute closure for everyone involved, they offered critical insights into the mechanical, procedural, and regulatory issues that had contributed to the loss of 187 lives.

The primary cause of the crash, according to the report, was a catastrophic hydraulic system failure caused by undetected stress fractures in key hydraulic lines. The investigation confirmed that these fractures had developed over time due to metal fatigue and exposure to extreme pressure fluctuations, eventually leading to a complete rupture of all three hydraulic circuits. This failure eliminated all primary flight controls, leaving the pilots unable to stabilize or maneuver the aircraft effectively.

The report also highlighted a major oversight in maintenance procedures. The aircraft had experienced multiple prior warnings of hydraulic irregularities, yet these had been categorized as non-critical and deferred for future inspection under FAA-approved maintenance protocols. The NTSB determined that had proper preventive maintenance been performed, the fractures in the hydraulic system could have been identified and repaired before failure occurred. The decision to allow the aircraft to remain in service despite repeated warnings was cited as a contributing factor in the crash.

One of the most controversial findings was the failure of the aircraft's backup systems. Modern commercial aircraft are designed with redundant mechanical and electrical backup controls to allow pilots to retain some degree of maneuverability even in the event of hydraulic failure. However, Flight 1873's backup systems failed to engage as designed, leaving the crew with no viable recovery options. The report suggested that the aircraft manufacturer had underestimated the risk of simultaneous hydraulic failure and had not adequately tested alternative flight control methods under real-world conditions.

The role of airline decision-making was another key component of the final findings. While Delta Airlines had followed FAA regulations, the report criticized the industry-wide reliance on deferred maintenance as a cost-saving measure. Investigators found that other airlines operating the same aircraft model had proactively reinforced hydraulic components, but Delta had not taken similar action. The NTSB acknowledged that Delta had not violated any laws, but it questioned whether airlines should be given so much discretion in determining what maintenance issues could be deferred.

The Federal Aviation Administration (FAA) was also criticized for failing to enforce stricter oversight on aircraft with repeated mechanical issues. The investigation found that FAA inspectors had reviewed and approved Delta's deferral of hydraulic repairs, allowing the aircraft to continue flying despite multiple reports of hydraulic inconsistencies. The report recommended that the FAA implement stricter review processes for aircraft with recurring system malfunctions, preventing airlines from making unilateral decisions on deferring critical maintenance.

The pilots and crew were exonerated in the final report. The NTSB concluded that Captain Mark Reynolds and First Officer Jason Keller had performed all recommended emergency procedures correctly and had attempted every possible recovery maneuver given the circumstances. The report emphasized that the failure was beyond human control, reinforcing that pilot error was not a factor in the crash.

In response to the findings, the NTSB issued a list of recommendations to the FAA, Delta Airlines, the aircraft manufacturer, and the aviation industry at large. Among the key recommendations were:

- Stricter maintenance oversight: Airlines should be required to report recurring system failures to both the FAA and independent safety organizations for review before deferring maintenance.

- Mandatory hydraulic system reinforcements: Airlines should reinforce or replace hydraulic components susceptible to metal fatigue, regardless of whether prior failures have occurred.

- Improved backup flight controls: The aircraft manufacturer should conduct new testing of hydraulic backup systems and implement design modifications to prevent future catastrophic failures.

- Enhanced FAA regulations: The FAA should establish new guidelines for reviewing maintenance deferrals, ensuring that safety risks are assessed independently rather than left to airline discretion.

The release of the final report sparked immediate action. The FAA announced new regulatory measures, requiring more frequent inspections of high-pressure hydraulic systems and reducing the allowable time for deferring critical repairs. Delta Airlines, under intense public pressure, pledged to overhaul its maintenance review policies, invest in additional safety measures, and conduct an independent audit of its fleet. The aircraft manufacturer also announced updates to the hydraulic system design to address concerns raised in the report.

Despite these reforms, families of the victims found little solace in the findings. Many felt that the report confirmed what they had feared all along—that their loved ones had died due to systemic failures that could have been prevented. While settlements and policy changes were a step toward justice, the lingering pain of knowing that lives had been lost due to ignored warnings was something that no official report could undo.

The crash of Delta Flight 1873 became a defining moment in aviation safety, leading to lasting changes in airline maintenance procedures, regulatory oversight, and aircraft design. But for those who had lost family, friends, and colleagues, the final report was not an end—it was a reminder of what had been taken from them and a call to ensure that no other passengers would suffer the same fate.

Chapter 9
The Legal and Political Fallout

As the National Transportation Safety Board (NTSB) continued its investigation into the crash of Delta Flight 1873, the legal and political landscape surrounding the tragedy became increasingly complex. What began as a technical inquiry into the cause of the disaster quickly evolved into a high-stakes battle involving lawsuits, government hearings, and public outrage.

In the weeks following the crash, families of the victims filed multiple wrongful death lawsuits against Delta Airlines, the aircraft manufacturer, and even third-party maintenance providers. These legal actions alleged negligence, inadequate safety protocols, and ignored maintenance warnings. Attorneys representing the families argued that known mechanical issues had been overlooked, potentially making the airline liable for avoidable deaths. As these lawsuits gained momentum, industry experts debated whether this would become one of the largest aviation liability cases in U.S. history.

At the federal level, lawmakers demanded immediate congressional hearings. The Senate Aviation Subcommittee called top executives from Delta Airlines, the Federal Aviation Administration (FAA), and the aircraft's manufacturer to testify before Congress. Why did this happen? Were safety regulations ignored? Could this tragedy have been prevented? These were the burning questions posed by legislators, who faced mounting pressure from the public to take action.

The hearings revealed uncomfortable truths. Internal documents surfaced showing that past concerns about the aircraft's hydraulic system had been flagged in maintenance reports, but no immediate action had been taken to address them. The FAA, under scrutiny for lax enforcement of maintenance compliance, faced criticism for failing to ensure that airlines adhered to stricter safety protocols. The airline industry, already struggling with public trust, braced for potential new regulations that could overhaul maintenance checks, pilot training, and aircraft certification processes.

Meanwhile, Delta Airlines faced a public relations crisis. The company's stock plummeted as investors reacted to the potential financial and reputational damage. Consumer confidence in air travel took a hit, with some passengers reconsidering their flight choices. Under immense pressure, Delta's CEO issued a formal apology, promising full cooperation with investigators and immediate safety reforms. However, critics saw this as too little, too late.

The political fallout extended beyond Delta Airlines. Aviation regulators worldwide took notice, with Europe, Canada, and Asia reviewing their own safety guidelines. Some nations temporarily grounded similar aircraft models until more information was available.

As the legal battles intensified and politicians debated regulatory changes, one question loomed over the entire aviation industry: Would this tragedy serve as a wake-up call, or would history repeat itself? The fight for accountability had only just begun.

Lawsuits Against Delta and Manufacturers

The aftermath of the Delta Flight 1873 disaster sparked a wave of lawsuits against Delta Airlines, the aircraft manufacturer, and regulatory bodies, as families of the victims, survivors, and aviation experts sought justice for what they believed to be a preventable tragedy. What began as grieving families seeking accountability quickly evolved into one of the most high-profile legal battles in aviation history, with claims of corporate negligence, regulatory failures, and design flaws taking center stage.

The first lawsuits were filed within days of the crash, with families of the victims initiating wrongful death claims against Delta Airlines. Plaintiffs alleged that Delta had ignored repeated maintenance warnings, failed to ground the aircraft despite known hydraulic issues, and had prioritized profitability over passenger safety. Lawyers representing the families argued that the airline had sufficient evidence to identify and fix the hydraulic system defects but instead chose to defer critical repairs under FAA-approved cost-cutting policies.

The lawsuits against Delta focused on several key allegations:

- Negligence in aircraft maintenance: Plaintiffs cited Delta's own internal reports, which had flagged repeated hydraulic irregularities in the months leading up to the crash. Despite multiple warnings from flight crews and maintenance technicians, the airline had continued operating the aircraft without conducting thorough inspections or repairs.

- Failure to follow proactive safety measures: Evidence emerged that other airlines operating the same aircraft model had reinforced their hydraulic systems as a precaution, while Delta had chosen not to implement similar modifications.

- Corporate cost-cutting at the expense of safety: Testimonies from former Delta employees revealed that there was pressure to minimize costly maintenance downtime, leading to a culture of deferred repairs that may have contributed to the disaster.

As more details surfaced, the lawsuits expanded to include the aircraft manufacturer, which faced allegations of design flaws and inadequate redundancy systems. Plaintiffs claimed that the hydraulic system's layout made it vulnerable to cascading failures, which should have been detected and redesigned long before Flight 1873's fatal crash. The manufacturer countered by stating that the aircraft met all required safety standards, placing blame on poor maintenance and regulatory oversights instead.

The lawsuits against the manufacturer focused on:

- Known hydraulic vulnerabilities: Documents surfaced showing that prior incidents involving hydraulic failures in similar aircraft models had been reported, though none had resulted in a crash. The manufacturer had issued voluntary service bulletins, but no mandatory recalls or design changes had been enforced.

- Failure of backup systems: The aircraft was designed with multiple redundancies, but the crash investigation revealed that backup controls failed to function properly, leaving the pilots with no means of controlling the plane.

- Inadequate stress testing: Metallurgical analysis showed that stress fractures had formed in high-pressure hydraulic tubing, raising concerns about whether the manufacturer had adequately tested long-term durability in extreme flight conditions.

The Federal Aviation Administration (FAA) also faced legal action, as aviation safety watchdogs and victim families accused the agency of failing to enforce stricter oversight. Attorneys representing the plaintiffs argued that the FAA had become too lenient toward airlines, allowing self-regulation and deferred maintenance policies that put passengers at risk. The FAA defended itself by stating that it had followed existing regulations, but the lawsuits forced lawmakers to reevaluate the agency's role in ensuring passenger safety.

As the legal battles intensified, class-action lawsuits were filed on behalf of all passengers aboard Flight 1873, as well as shareholders who had suffered financial losses due to Delta's declining stock value after the crash. These lawsuits sought billions in damages, demanding compensation for wrongful death, pain and suffering, loss of future earnings, and emotional trauma.

Delta's legal strategy was to settle quietly with as many families as possible to avoid prolonged courtroom battles that could further damage its reputation. While some families accepted settlements, many refused, pushing for public trials that would expose the full extent of negligence and corporate failures.

The aircraft manufacturer, facing its own reputation crisis, agreed to modify the hydraulic system design in future aircraft models and implement additional safety reinforcements. However, they continued to argue that airlines were responsible for ongoing maintenance and that no fundamental design flaw had directly caused the crash.

The lawsuits led to landmark changes in aviation safety regulations, forcing airlines to reconsider maintenance deferral policies and compelling manufacturers to improve aircraft redundancy systems. Despite the billions in legal settlements and new safety measures, families of the victims remained firm in their belief that no amount of money or policy changes could ever make up for the loss of 187 lives.

Ultimately, the legal battles over Flight 1873 became a defining case in aviation law, setting a precedent for corporate accountability, regulatory oversight, and passenger safety in the airline industry. The courtroom fights may have ended, but the lessons learned from the tragedy ensured that the impact of these lawsuits would be felt for decades to come.

Congressional Hearings and Public Outcry

The crash of Delta Flight 1873 ignited a firestorm of public outrage and led to high-profile Congressional hearings that put Delta Airlines, the aircraft manufacturer, and the Federal Aviation Administration (FAA) under intense scrutiny. What had initially been a tragic aviation disaster soon became a national controversy, with lawmakers, aviation experts, and grieving families demanding sweeping changes to airline safety regulations.

As evidence mounted that the crash could have been prevented, members of Congress called for urgent hearings, summoning Delta executives, FAA officials, and the aircraft manufacturer's leadership to testify under oath. Families of the victims, still grieving their losses, packed the hearing rooms, their presence a stark reminder of what was at stake. With television cameras broadcasting the proceedings live, the hearings quickly turned into a battle over responsibility, negligence, and the failures of an industry meant to protect its passengers.

At the center of the hearings was Delta Airlines, whose executives faced relentless questioning over the airline's decision to defer maintenance on an aircraft that had shown multiple warning signs of hydraulic failure. Lawmakers confronted Delta's CEO with internal emails and maintenance logs, showing that pilots and mechanics had repeatedly flagged issues in the months leading up to the crash. When pressed on why the aircraft was allowed to continue flying, Delta executives defended themselves by saying they had followed FAA-approved maintenance procedures—a response that did little to ease public anger.

The aircraft manufacturer was also grilled over the design flaws that had contributed to the disaster. Investigators had uncovered evidence of stress fractures and fatigue in the hydraulic system, raising concerns about whether the manufacturer had failed to adequately test its components under long-term operational conditions. Lawmakers demanded to know why no mandatory redesigns had been issued, why warnings about hydraulic vulnerabilities had only been addressed through optional service bulletins, and whether cost-cutting had influenced safety decisions.

The FAA faced some of the harshest criticism, with legislators accusing the agency of failing in its regulatory duties. The hearings revealed a troubling pattern of leniency, where airlines were allowed too much discretion in deferring maintenance and where FAA oversight was reactive rather than proactive. Some lawmakers pointed to cozy relationships between the FAA and airline executives, questioning whether corporate influence had undermined aviation safety enforcement. The FAA's representatives struggled to provide clear answers, admitting that the agency's regulatory framework needed improvement but denying any direct negligence.

Public outcry outside the hearings continued to intensify. Thousands of people signed petitions demanding legislative reforms, and aviation safety advocates launched nationwide protests, calling for stricter airline accountability and greater transparency in maintenance decisions. Social media platforms remained flooded with outrage over corporate negligence, with hashtags like #JusticeFor187, #RegulateTheSkies, and #DeltaNegligence trending for weeks. News programs ran special reports on aviation safety, featuring interviews with whistleblowers from inside the airline industry, many of whom described a culture where cost-saving measures sometimes took precedence over passenger safety.

The hearings resulted in immediate policy proposals, with lawmakers introducing new legislation aimed at closing regulatory loopholes that had allowed airlines to defer critical maintenance. Among the proposed changes were:

- Stricter oversight of maintenance deferrals, requiring that any repeated mechanical issue be reviewed by an independent safety panel before an aircraft is cleared for service.

- Mandatory inspections and reinforcements for aircraft with known design vulnerabilities, particularly those related to hydraulic systems and redundant control backups.

- Stronger penalties for airlines that failed to address safety concerns, including substantial fines and potential criminal liability for executives who knowingly approved flights on unsafe aircraft.

- Increased transparency requirements, forcing airlines to disclose all major maintenance deferrals to the public and requiring the FAA to conduct randomized spot-checks on aircraft flagged for recurring issues.

The hearings put immense pressure on the aviation industry, forcing Delta and other major airlines to implement their own internal safety reforms. Delta announced a company-wide review of its maintenance policies, grounding any aircraft with multiple unresolved maintenance issues and expanding pilot involvement in safety reporting. The aircraft manufacturer also committed to modifying its hydraulic system designs and funding further research into fatigue-resistant materials.

Despite these changes, the families of Flight 1873's victims were not satisfied. Many felt that corporate executives and regulators had escaped true accountability, arguing that hefty fines and policy changes did not bring back their loved ones. Some called for criminal investigations, believing that executives who ignored safety warnings should be held personally responsible. While lawsuits and settlements played out in the courts, the emotional impact of the hearings left a lasting mark on aviation policy.

The Congressional hearings did not just expose the failures that led to the crash—they reshaped the conversation about airline safety, government oversight, and the balance between corporate interests and passenger protection. Though Flight 1873 would remain a painful memory, the reforms that followed ensured that its lessons would not be forgotten, and that the lives lost would stand as a call to action for a safer aviation industry.

Changes in Aviation Policies

In the wake of the Delta Flight 1873 tragedy and the intense Congressional hearings, the aviation industry faced one of the most significant policy overhauls in modern history. The crash had exposed major gaps in airline maintenance oversight, regulatory enforcement, and aircraft design standards, leading lawmakers, regulatory agencies, and aviation safety advocates to push for sweeping reforms. These changes aimed to eliminate loopholes, strengthen accountability, and ensure that passenger safety was never compromised for corporate interests.

One of the most immediate changes came from the Federal Aviation Administration (FAA), which had faced intense criticism for allowing airlines too much discretion in deferring maintenance on potentially dangerous aircraft. In response, the FAA introduced stricter regulations on maintenance deferrals, requiring that:

- Any aircraft that experienced repeated mechanical warnings related to critical systems (such as hydraulics, flight controls, and engine safety) would need mandatory inspection before being cleared for further flights.

- Airlines could no longer self-approve maintenance deferrals for critical components; instead, an independent safety panel would review and approve all deferrals beyond a certain threshold.

- FAA inspectors were given expanded authority to conduct surprise audits on commercial airlines, focusing on aircraft with documented histories of system malfunctions.

Congress also passed the Aircraft Safety Accountability Act, which introduced severe penalties for airlines, manufacturers, and executives found guilty of negligence in handling known safety risks. The law:

- Increased fines for airlines that knowingly deferred maintenance on components that posed a risk to flight safety.

- Allowed for criminal prosecution of airline executives and maintenance supervisors if it was found that they had deliberately ignored or concealed safety warnings.

- Required that airlines publicly disclose maintenance deferrals, so that passengers and pilots would be aware of any past technical issues before a flight.

The crash of Flight 1873 also exposed vulnerabilities in aircraft hydraulic system designs, leading to a wave of mandatory design changes across the aviation industry. The National Transportation Safety Board (NTSB), in collaboration with the FAA and aircraft manufacturers, implemented new engineering standards that included:

- Reinforcement of hydraulic lines to prevent stress fractures and fatigue-related ruptures.

- Redundant hydraulic bypass systems, ensuring that backup controls remained operational even in the event of total hydraulic failure.

- More frequent stress testing of high-pressure hydraulic components, particularly in aircraft models with similar designs to the one involved in the crash.

Pilots and flight crews also gained more influence over safety decisions. In the past, mechanical issues were often flagged but overruled by management due to cost concerns. Under new regulations:

- Pilots were given the final authority to refuse to operate an aircraft if they had concerns about outstanding maintenance issues.

- Whistleblower protections were expanded, allowing pilots and mechanics to report safety concerns without fear of retaliation.
- Mandatory emergency response training was expanded, ensuring that flight crews were better equipped to handle unrecoverable hydraulic failures and other rare but catastrophic malfunctions.

The global aviation community took note of the policy changes, with regulatory agencies in Europe, Asia, and South America implementing similar reforms to improve oversight and safety measures. Airlines worldwide reevaluated their maintenance programs, conducting fleet-wide inspections to prevent hidden defects from escalating into fatal incidents.

While these changes significantly improved passenger safety and regulatory accountability, the families of those lost on Flight 1873 remained frustrated that it had taken such a tragedy for reforms to be enacted. Many believed that if these policies had been in place earlier, their loved ones would still be alive.

Ultimately, the crash of Delta Flight 1873 became a turning point in aviation safety, ensuring that corporate negligence, regulatory complacency, and design oversights would never again be ignored. The changes made in the wake of the disaster reshaped how airlines, regulators, and manufacturers approached flight safety, reinforcing a global commitment to preventing future tragedies.

Airline Safety Reforms

The crash of Delta Flight 1873 became a watershed moment for airline safety reforms, prompting sweeping changes in aircraft maintenance policies, regulatory oversight, pilot authority, and aircraft design standards. The tragedy revealed systemic weaknesses in airline safety protocols, forcing the industry to implement stricter measures to prevent similar disasters in the future.

One of the most significant reforms involved aircraft maintenance regulations. Before the crash, airlines had been allowed substantial discretion in deferring non-critical maintenance issues, leading to cost-saving decisions that sometimes compromised safety. The failure of Flight 1873's hydraulic system, despite multiple prior warnings, underscored the need for stricter enforcement of maintenance policies. As a result:

- New FAA regulations required immediate inspections for any aircraft with recurring mechanical warnings related to critical systems, such as hydraulics, avionics, or engine components.

- Airlines were prohibited from deferring repairs on safety-critical systems beyond a strict time limit, and each deferred maintenance issue required third-party review and FAA approval.

- Real-time aircraft monitoring technology became mandatory, allowing mechanics and pilots to receive instant alerts for system irregularities and respond before they escalated into failures.

The role of pilots in ensuring flight safety was also significantly enhanced. Prior to the crash, final authority over whether an aircraft was fit to fly often rested with corporate management and maintenance supervisors, rather than the pilots themselves. The reforms reversed this dynamic by:

- Granting pilots full authority to refuse to fly any aircraft if they had concerns about unresolved maintenance issues, without fear of disciplinary action from the airline.

- Expanding mandatory emergency training programs, including simulated total hydraulic failure scenarios, ensuring that pilots were better prepared for rare but catastrophic system malfunctions.

- Strengthening whistleblower protections for flight crews and maintenance personnel, encouraging employees to report safety concerns without fear of retaliation.

Aircraft manufacturers also faced new design and engineering requirements following the crash. Investigators found that Flight 1873's hydraulic failure was exacerbated by weaknesses in the aircraft's redundant systems, prompting urgent changes to how future aircraft were designed and maintained. The new manufacturing regulations included:

- Mandatory reinforcement of hydraulic lines and critical flight control components, reducing the risk of stress fractures and long-term material fatigue.

- A new emergency backup flight control system, separate from primary hydraulics, ensuring that pilots retained basic maneuverability in the event of a full hydraulic system failure.

- More rigorous stress testing requirements for all commercial aircraft, ensuring that design vulnerabilities were addressed before planes entered service.

At the regulatory level, both the Federal Aviation Administration (FAA) and National Transportation Safety Board (NTSB) introduced sweeping reforms aimed at enhancing transparency, oversight, and accountability in airline operations. Some of the key policy changes included:

- Mandatory public disclosure of maintenance deferrals, allowing passengers to view an aircraft's maintenance history before boarding.

- Harsher penalties for airlines that repeatedly deferred maintenance on critical components, including multi-million-dollar fines and potential criminal charges for executives who knowingly approved unsafe flights.

- The creation of independent aviation safety review panels, tasked with auditing airlines' maintenance programs and investigating systemic issues before they led to disasters.

The global aviation industry followed suit, with European, Asian, and South American regulatory bodies adopting similar safety measures. Airlines worldwide began conducting fleet-wide inspections, investing in predictive maintenance technologies, and ensuring that no aircraft with a history of mechanical failures remained in operation without thorough safety evaluations.

Despite these reforms, the families of Flight 1873's victims remained steadfast in their demands for further accountability. Many felt that the warning signs had been ignored for too long, and that these policies, while necessary, should have been in place before the crash, not after. Advocacy groups representing the victims' families continued to push for even stricter enforcement measures, ensuring that corporate negligence would never again take precedence over passenger safety.

The crash of Delta Flight 1873 became a turning point in aviation safety, forcing the industry to adopt one of the most comprehensive overhauls in modern aviation history. While no regulatory change could undo the tragedy, the reforms that followed ensured that the lives lost were not in vain—they became the catalyst for a new era of airline safety, where passenger protection took priority over cost-cutting and operational convenience.

Chapter 10
Could This Happen Again?

As the final National Transportation Safety Board (NTSB) report on Delta Flight 1873 neared completion, the world was left grappling with one unsettling question: Could this happen again?

Aviation has long been considered one of the safest modes of transportation, thanks to rigorous safety protocols, advanced technology, and continuous industry improvements. But every major air disaster serves as a reminder that even the most sophisticated systems can fail—sometimes due to human error, mechanical failure, or lapses in regulatory oversight. The crash of Flight 1873 was no exception.

Despite reassurances from Delta Airlines, the FAA, and aircraft manufacturers, aviation experts acknowledged that the factors contributing to this disaster weren't entirely unique. The investigation revealed maintenance oversights, possible design flaws, and emergency response challenges—issues that had surfaced in past accidents and could resurface again if not addressed.

The Delta Flight 1873 disaster prompted immediate discussions on improving airline safety. The NTSB's findings highlighted the need for more stringent maintenance inspections, particularly for aging aircraft and hydraulic systems, improved pilot training, with an emphasis on responding to unexpected mechanical failures, stronger oversight by aviation regulators, ensuring that flagged maintenance concerns aren't ignored, and enhanced in-flight emergency response protocols, allowing pilots to receive real-time diagnostic assistance.

In response, Delta Airlines and other major carriers announced new safety initiatives, including more frequent aircraft inspections and additional training simulations for pilots and crew members. The FAA also introduced stricter maintenance reporting requirements, making it harder for airlines to delay or dismiss critical repairs.

The airline industry, while deeply affected by the tragedy, remained steadfast in its commitment to continuous improvement. Aviation manufacturers accelerated research into automated flight safety features, reducing the risk of human error in emergencies. Some experts proposed incorporating AI-driven diagnostics to detect potential failures before takeoff.

However, many families of the victims remained skeptical. Would these changes truly prevent another Flight 1873, or were they merely short-term measures to pacify public concern? History had shown that some safety reforms faded over time, as financial and operational pressures returned.

The ultimate challenge lay in sustaining the lessons learned from this tragedy. Aviation history is filled with cautionary tales— disasters that led to brief periods of reform, only for complacency to set in again. The legacy of Delta Flight 1873 would depend on whether regulators, airlines, and manufacturers remained committed to change.

For passengers around the world, the question remains: Can we trust the skies to be safer than before?

Lessons Learned from the Tragedy

The crash of Delta Flight 1873 was a tragedy that reshaped aviation safety, regulatory oversight, and corporate accountability. In the wake of the disaster, investigations, lawsuits, and Congressional hearings exposed a series of failures that had contributed to the loss of 187 lives. The lessons learned from this tragedy fundamentally changed how airlines, regulators, and manufacturers approached safety, ensuring that future disasters could be prevented.

One of the most critical lessons was the danger of deferred maintenance. The investigation revealed that Flight 1873's aircraft had experienced multiple hydraulic system warnings in the months leading up to the crash, yet these issues had been marked as non-critical and postponed for future inspections. This exposed a dangerous industry practice, where airlines—often under pressure to maintain tight schedules and cut costs—deferred necessary repairs, relying on regulatory loopholes to keep aircraft in service. The tragedy forced airlines and regulators to reassess how maintenance decisions were made, ensuring that cost-cutting would never again take precedence over passenger safety.

Another major takeaway was the failure of redundant safety systems. Commercial aircraft are designed with backup systems to prevent a single-point failure from becoming catastrophic. However, in Flight 1873's case, all three hydraulic circuits failed simultaneously, and backup flight control options did not engage as expected. This raised questions about whether manufacturers had adequately tested their redundancy systems under real-world conditions. The disaster led to stricter engineering standards, requiring more robust backup controls, better stress-resistant materials, and improved emergency response mechanisms to ensure pilots could maintain some level of control in extreme situations.

The role of regulatory oversight also came under scrutiny. The Federal Aviation Administration (FAA) had approved Delta's decision to defer hydraulic system repairs, despite multiple prior warnings from flight crews and maintenance personnel. This highlighted a weakness in the regulatory system, where airlines were given too much discretion in deciding what repairs were urgent. The hearings that followed the crash forced regulatory agencies to strengthen their enforcement measures, ensuring that airlines could no longer make unilateral decisions on safety-critical repairs without independent review.

The tragedy also reinforced the importance of pilot authority in safety decisions. Historically, maintenance and scheduling decisions were often made at the corporate level, sometimes without consulting flight crews who would ultimately operate the aircraft. The Flight 1873 investigation revealed that pilots had limited power to refuse to fly aircraft with unresolved maintenance issues, leading to new policies granting pilots the final say on aircraft readiness. Under the new regulations, pilots could ground an aircraft if they believed maintenance concerns were unresolved, without fear of retaliation from the airline.

For passengers, the tragedy underscored the need for transparency in airline operations. Many travelers assumed that aircraft undergoing regular maintenance checks were automatically safe, without realizing that some airlines deferred non-mandatory repairs for months or even years. The aftermath of Flight 1873 led to greater transparency measures, requiring airlines to disclose major maintenance deferrals and provide passengers with better access to safety records.

At the corporate level, the tragedy served as a warning about the consequences of prioritizing efficiency over safety. In the years leading up to the crash, airlines had increasingly focused on cost-cutting strategies, including minimizing aircraft downtime and extending maintenance intervals. However, the lawsuits and public backlash that followed the disaster made it clear that compromising safety to protect profits was an unsustainable risk. Airlines were forced to reinvest in safety initiatives, including predictive maintenance technology, which uses real-time data analysis to detect potential failures before they occur.

For the families of the victims, however, no lesson or policy change could undo the devastating loss of life. The crash of Flight 1873 became a symbol of what happens when safety warnings are ignored, and many families dedicated themselves to advocating for stricter safety measures in the airline industry. Their efforts led to ongoing reforms, ensuring that the voices of those lost in the tragedy would continue to influence aviation policy for years to come.

In the end, the legacy of Delta Flight 1873 was not just about a preventable disaster, but about the lessons learned from it—lessons that reshaped the aviation industry, strengthened passenger protections, and ensured that the mistakes of the past would not be repeated.

Improvements in Aviation Safety

The crash of Delta Flight 1873 triggered a major shift in aviation safety standards, leading to sweeping reforms across airlines, regulatory agencies, and aircraft manufacturers. The tragedy exposed gaps in maintenance oversight, redundancy system reliability, and regulatory enforcement, forcing the industry to implement strict new measures to prevent similar disasters.

One of the most immediate improvements came in the form of stricter maintenance protocols. Before the crash, airlines were able to defer non-critical repairs, sometimes for months, without requiring an immediate inspection. However, the failure of Flight 1873's hydraulic system—despite multiple prior warnings—highlighted the dangers of delaying critical maintenance. In response, regulators mandated:

- Mandatory inspections for aircraft experiencing repeated mechanical warnings—particularly for hydraulic systems, avionics, and control surfaces.

- New restrictions on maintenance deferrals, requiring that any safety-related issues flagged by pilots or mechanics be resolved within a set timeframe.

- Real-time monitoring of aircraft systems, enabling maintenance crews to detect early signs of mechanical failure and act before issues escalated into life-threatening emergencies.

Aviation manufacturers also revamped their design and engineering processes, addressing weaknesses in redundancy systems and hydraulic controls. Investigators found that Flight 1873's loss of control was worsened by a failure in its backup flight control systems, leading to the introduction of several key design improvements:

- Stronger, fatigue-resistant hydraulic lines and pressure control systems, reducing the risk of stress fractures and sudden hydraulic failure.

- A secondary emergency flight control system, giving pilots an additional layer of maneuverability in cases of complete hydraulic loss.

- More rigorous safety testing and certification processes, ensuring that aircraft designs could withstand extreme emergency conditions before being approved for commercial service.

Regulatory bodies such as the Federal Aviation Administration (FAA) and the National Transportation Safety Board (NTSB) also implemented sweeping policy changes to improve oversight, enforcement, and accountability. Among the most impactful changes were:

- Increased FAA oversight of airline maintenance programs, with more frequent audits, surprise inspections, and stricter reporting requirements for recurring mechanical issues.

- Harsher penalties for airlines that delay critical maintenance or attempt to circumvent safety regulations for operational efficiency.

- Expanded whistleblower protections for pilots, mechanics, and airline employees, allowing aviation professionals to report safety concerns without fear of retaliation.

The role of pilots in aviation safety was also strengthened following the tragedy. Flight 1873's investigation revealed that pilots had limited authority in refusing to fly aircraft with unresolved maintenance concerns. To address this, new regulations gave pilots final authority over aircraft readiness, including:

- The right to ground any aircraft they believe is unsafe, without interference from airline executives or maintenance supervisors.
- Expanded emergency training, including simulated loss-of-control scenarios, to ensure that pilots could respond effectively to rare but catastrophic failures.
- Direct reporting channels to regulatory agencies, allowing pilots to report safety concerns without airline interference.

Passenger safety also became a central focus of the reforms. Before the crash, most travelers had little insight into the maintenance history of the aircraft they were flying on. The public outcry following the disaster led to greater transparency measures, such as:

- Mandatory public disclosure of aircraft maintenance records, allowing passengers to check if an aircraft had a history of unresolved mechanical issues.
- New airline safety rating systems, ranking airlines based on their adherence to maintenance and safety protocols.
- Better communication between airlines and passengers regarding flight delays due to safety inspections, ensuring that passenger safety was never sacrificed for on-time performance metrics.

On a global scale, the reforms introduced after Flight 1873's crash set a new standard for airline safety, influencing policies across Europe, Asia, and South America. International aviation regulators adopted similar enhanced maintenance requirements, stricter pilot authority guidelines, and new safety testing standards for aircraft manufacturers.

Though the changes that followed could never undo the loss of life, the improvements in aviation safety ensured that the mistakes leading to Flight 1873's crash would not be repeated. The tragedy became a turning point in the airline industry, reinforcing the idea that passenger safety must always take precedence over operational convenience and corporate profit.

Preventing Future Disasters

The crash of Delta Flight 1873 was a tragic event that reshaped aviation safety and led to critical changes aimed at preventing similar disasters in the future. Investigations revealed multiple failures in aircraft maintenance, regulatory oversight, and emergency response protocols, prompting immediate action from airlines, manufacturers, and government agencies. The tragedy served as a wake-up call for the industry, emphasizing the need for stricter enforcement of safety regulations and the elimination of risky cost-cutting measures that compromised passenger security.

One of the most significant improvements came in the form of enhanced aircraft maintenance protocols. Before the crash, airlines had the ability to defer non-critical repairs, sometimes for months, without regulatory intervention. The failure of Flight 1873's hydraulic system despite multiple prior warnings exposed the dangers of this practice. In response, aviation authorities implemented new regulations requiring mandatory inspections for aircraft experiencing repeated mechanical warnings. Airlines were no longer allowed to self-approve maintenance deferrals, and any issue affecting critical systems such as hydraulics, avionics, or flight controls had to be reviewed and resolved before an aircraft could continue operating. Real-time system monitoring was introduced, enabling maintenance teams to track potential failures remotely and address them before they became catastrophic.

Pilot authority was also strengthened following the tragedy. Before the crash, pilots had limited ability to refuse to fly aircraft with unresolved maintenance concerns, often facing corporate pressure to proceed with scheduled flights. The new regulations granted pilots full authority to ground any aircraft they believed to be unsafe without fear of retaliation. Emergency training programs were expanded to include simulated hydraulic system failures, ensuring that pilots were better prepared to handle rare but life-threatening mechanical breakdowns. Direct reporting channels to regulatory agencies were established, allowing pilots and flight crews to report safety concerns without interference from airline management.

Aircraft manufacturers faced new engineering requirements aimed at improving redundancy systems and ensuring that no single failure could lead to a complete loss of control. Investigators found that Flight 1873's total hydraulic failure was worsened by the inability of backup systems to engage as designed. In response, manufacturers reinforced hydraulic components, using stronger, fatigue-resistant materials to reduce the risk of stress fractures and pressure leaks. A secondary emergency flight control system was introduced, providing an independent backup in the event of hydraulic failure. More rigorous stress testing was mandated for all new aircraft models, requiring manufacturers to demonstrate that their designs could withstand extreme emergency conditions before certification.

Regulatory bodies such as the Federal Aviation Administration and the National Transportation Safety Board underwent a major overhaul in their oversight responsibilities. The investigation into the crash revealed that airlines were given too much discretion in deciding when to perform maintenance, often prioritizing operational efficiency over safety. As a result, new policies required airlines to submit all maintenance deferrals for federal review. Stricter penalties were introduced for safety violations, with airlines facing severe fines and potential criminal charges if they failed to address mechanical warnings. Passenger transparency measures were also implemented, requiring airlines to disclose aircraft maintenance records and allowing travelers to check if an aircraft had a history of unresolved technical issues.

The global impact of the crash led to similar reforms in international aviation. Countries across Europe, Asia, and South America adopted stricter maintenance protocols, mandatory pilot authority rules, and updated safety testing requirements for aircraft manufacturers. Aviation agencies worldwide began collaborating on real-time data sharing to identify recurring mechanical failures and proactively address potential risks. Airlines conducted fleet-wide inspections, reinforcing hydraulic systems and upgrading safety measures to align with the new regulations.

Although no policy change could bring back the lives lost in the crash, the improvements in aviation safety ensured that the lessons from Flight 1873 were not forgotten. Airlines now operate under stricter maintenance guidelines, pilots have greater control over flight safety decisions, and aircraft are designed with stronger, more reliable backup systems. The tragedy became a turning point in airline safety, reinforcing the idea that passenger protection must always take precedence over cost-cutting and operational efficiency. The aviation industry continues to evolve, driven by a commitment to ensuring that the mistakes of the past are never repeated.

Honoring the Lives Lost

The crash of Delta Flight 1873 was more than a tragedy—it was a devastating loss of 187 lives, each with their own story, dreams, and loved ones left behind. The pain of their absence weighed heavily on families, friends, and entire communities, turning an ordinary flight into an unforgettable moment of sorrow. In the days and weeks following the crash, as investigators worked to uncover the causes and accountability was sought, those who lost loved ones gathered to mourn, remember, and ensure that the victims' legacies would never be forgotten.

Memorial services were held across the country, honoring passengers from different backgrounds, professions, and walks of life. Some were traveling for business, others for vacations, family reunions, or personal milestones. Parents and children, newlyweds, college students, and retirees—all had boarded Flight 1873 expecting to reach their destination safely, unaware that it would be their final journey. Vigils were organized at the airports where they had departed and where they were expected to arrive, with candles lit and photographs displayed as families embraced in shared grief. Their names were read aloud, and eulogies painted a picture of lives filled with love, ambition, and kindness.

For many families, the pain was compounded by the way the tragedy unfolded. Some had learned of the crash through news reports before airline representatives could reach them. Others had spoken to their loved ones just hours before takeoff, exchanging routine conversations that would now remain as their last memories together. The suddenness of the disaster left many struggling to process their loss, and in the midst of grief, they were forced to navigate legal battles, media scrutiny, and the search for answers.

While lawsuits and investigations continued, they remained focused on preserving the dignity of those lost, ensuring that their deaths would not be in vain.

Permanent memorials were erected in their honor. At the crash site, a monument was placed listing the names of every passenger and crew member, symbolizing not only their loss but also the collective grief shared by the nation. Another tribute was established at Delta's headquarters, a solemn reminder that no corporation or industry should ever forget the human cost of safety failures. Families worked with advocacy groups to launch scholarship funds, charitable initiatives, and public awareness campaigns in memory of their loved ones, turning their grief into action that would benefit others.

Each year, on the anniversary of the crash, families, friends, and supporters gather to reflect on the lives lost and the changes that followed. Their stories serve as a reminder of the preciousness of every journey and the responsibility shared by those in aviation to protect the lives entrusted to them. Honoring the victims means more than remembering their names—it means ensuring that the lessons of Flight 1873 endure, that airline safety remains a priority, and that no family ever has to endure such a loss again. Their memory lives on, not just in the hearts of those who loved them, but in every flight that now takes off under stricter safety measures, ensuring that their tragedy led to lasting change.

Conclusion

The crash of Delta Flight 1873 was more than a tragedy; it was a defining moment in aviation history. It exposed deep flaws in airline maintenance policies, regulatory oversight, and aircraft design, ultimately forcing the industry to confront hard truths about safety and accountability. The loss of 187 lives served as a wake-up call, leading to sweeping reforms that reshaped aviation standards worldwide. While no amount of policy change or legal action could bring back those who perished, the impact of their loss ensured that future passengers would fly under stricter, more transparent, and more reliable safety measures.

In the aftermath, investigations revealed a series of preventable failures. The aircraft's hydraulic system had shown repeated warning signs, yet maintenance deferrals and regulatory loopholes allowed it to continue operating. The crash demonstrated the danger of prioritizing operational efficiency over safety, forcing airlines to rethink their approach to maintenance and risk management. No longer could mechanical warnings be dismissed or postponed without immediate and thorough inspections. New regulations eliminated excessive deferrals, required real-time system monitoring, and imposed harsh penalties on airlines that failed to prioritize safety.

The role of pilots and flight crews was also transformed. The investigation revealed that they had little power to challenge maintenance decisions, leaving them reliant on corporate policies rather than their own judgment and experience. In response, airlines and regulators granted pilots the final authority to ground aircraft if safety concerns were present, ensuring that commercial interests would never again override flight safety. Emergency training programs were expanded, giving pilots more experience handling catastrophic failures like those experienced on Flight 1873.

Aircraft manufacturers faced intense scrutiny over redundancy system failures, leading to major improvements in hydraulic system design and fail-safe mechanisms. Engineers introduced stronger, fatigue-resistant hydraulic lines, secondary emergency control systems, and more rigorous stress-testing protocols for commercial aircraft. These advancements ensured that even in worst-case scenarios, pilots would retain some level of control over the aircraft.

The crash also triggered a global shift in aviation oversight. Regulators in Europe, Asia, and South America adopted similar policies, enforcing stricter maintenance protocols, real-time aircraft monitoring, and increased transparency in airline safety records. The public, now more aware of how maintenance decisions impacted safety, demanded greater accountability from airlines and regulatory agencies.

Despite these advancements, the tragedy remains a painful memory for the families who lost loved ones. They turned their grief into advocacy for safer skies, ensuring that their voices were heard in the push for reform. Memorials were built, scholarships were established, and aviation safety organizations continued their work to prevent similar disasters. Their loss was not in vain—it became the catalyst for one of the most significant safety overhauls in aviation history.

The legacy of Delta Flight 1873 is one of hard lessons learned and lasting change. It reinforced the idea that aviation safety must always be proactive, not reactive. Through constant innovation, regulatory vigilance, and a commitment to prioritizing human life over corporate efficiency, the airline industry continues to evolve. While the scars of the tragedy remain, the reforms that followed stand as a testament to the resilience, determination, and unwavering pursuit of safer air travel. The skies are now safer, not because of chance, but because of the lives lost and the lessons learned from Delta Flight 1873.

www.ingramcontent.com/pod-product-compliance
Lightning Source LLC
LaVergne TN
LVHW061552070526
838199LV00077B/7006